LIVING WITH AUTISM

FIONA MARSHALL has written widely on health, psychology and parenting. She is the author of eight books, six of them for Sheldon Press, and also a novel.

Overcoming Common Problems Series

For a full list of titles please contact
Sheldon Press, Marylebone Road, London NW1 4DU

Overcoming Common Problems

Living with Autism

Fiona Marshall

First published in Great Britain in 2004 by
Sheldon Press
1 Marylebone Road
London NW1 4DU

British Library Cataloguing-in-Publication Data

A catalogue record for this book is available from the British Library

ISBN 0–85969–911–0

1 3 5 7 9 10 8 6 4 2

Typeset by Deltatype Limited, Birkenhead, Merseyside
Printed in Great Britain by Biddles Ltd
www.biddles.co.uk

Contents

Acknowledgements

I am indebted to the pioneering work of Leo Kanner, Hans Asperger and Dr Lorna Wing.

Wonderful sources of support and information include the National Autistic Society in the UK and the Autism Society of America (ASA) in the USA.

My special thanks to Jim Sinclair and June Gill for sharing their experiences of autism and to all the other families who helped to make this book possible.

Note: In this book 'autism' and 'autistic' are used as general terms which also denote Asperger syndrome as well as the entire autistic spectrum.

Introduction

Picture this. You're in a crowd, yet you avoid eye contact. If someone ventures to address a friendly remark, you may start or ignore the speaker. You do your best to remain enclosed within your own world, hoping desperately to reach the safety of your own home environment soon. Maybe you're feeling too hot and can't breathe comfortably. The tension around you is palpable. You protect your shell as best you can with a book, magazine, personal stereo, crossword puzzle. Are you autistic? No, you're using public transport – stuck on a train, bus or tube in the rush hour, trying to survive in a hopelessly overcrowded and uncomfortable environment.

Solipsistic, isolated individuals battling against the overpowering forces of the community; it's an autistic world. The difference is of course that most of us can switch our sociability on and off at will, but is there something in the structure of our society that helps explain our fascination with autism?

Autism, or autistic spectrum disorder (ASD), is a high-profile disorder that is threatening to assume epidemic proportions. Whether there is a real rise in autism or we are just better at recognizing it, autism seems to be here to stay, and demanding its fair share of benefits, education and support.

Until the 1960s, autism was viewed as a relatively rare disorder. Over the past few years, professionals' recognition of autism has soared. Equally, press coverage has boomed, not just of controversial issues, such as the possibility of a link between autism and vaccines, but serious, in-depth explorations of a disorder that can vary a great deal in its severity and effects.

Most people have heard of autism and have some idea of what it is – even if this is just a folk mythology of autism. People's ideas range widely, from grim reports of suicidal parents pushed too far by the stress of having an autistic child, to near-fairy tales of 'savants' who can draw brilliantly or are mathematics geniuses.

Compare autism, which affects an estimated 1 in 1000, with another, much more common, neurological disorder, epilepsy, which affects 1 in 200. Autism has caught the cultural imagination in a way

vii

that epilepsy, for all its prevalence, has not. Maybe the archetype of the individual or loner has deep resonances for our society.

It has been said that the central problem of those with autism is that they lack a sense of context, that they have experiences, but not the ability to place those experiences. How far are those with autism different from the rest of us in this? Is autism a metaphor for our own cultural twenty-first century uncertainty? Autism raises piquant questions about how far it is possible to enter or understand the world of others, questions that have increasing relevance in an ever more crowded world.

What is autism? Once condemned as a result of cold parenting, autism is now recognized as being a neurological disorder that affects the way a person communicates and relates to other people. Studies of abnormalities in several regions of the autistic brain suggest that the disorder results from a disruption in early foetal brain development. Recent studies also strongly suggest that some people have a genetic predisposition to autism, although for some children, environmental factors also may play a role in actually precipitating it.

What is known for certain is that autism is not a psychological disorder, as was at first believed by the German psychiatrist Leo Kanner at the Johns Hopkins Hospital, Baltimore. He was the first to publish a report on autism in 1943, 'Autistic Disturbances of Affective Contact', which placed 'Kanner's autism' in the medical textbooks for some years.

Asperger syndrome, so-called high-functioning autism, followed the next year (1944) when Hans Asperger published 'Autistic Psychopathy in Childhood'. His work did not become known in the UK until the late 1980s, after autism expert Lorna Wing described the syndrome fully in a paper on Asperger syndrome in 1981 – the year after Hans Asperger's death.

Autism was documented well before this, however, surfacing in early myths and stories of changelings. Indeed, Dr Wing suggests that stories of fairies stealing human babies, leaving changelings behind, are early references to autism. (These stories have also been linked with the doppelganger phenomenon, perhaps another concept that hints at the 'otherness' at the heart of autism. These concern a twin who does not exist, a being who looks like the original person but lacks their essential essence. These provoke the kinds of disturbing feelings that play a part in the grief of some parents when their thus far normal child is diagnosed with this profound developmental disorder.)

Other stories would also seem to chart autism through the mists of history. One is the theory that Brother Juniper, a disciple of St Francis of Assisi, was autistic. He was literal in his obedience, showed stereotypical behaviour and may have suffered seizures. In the early 1800s, Victor the 'Wild Boy of Aveyron' was found living wild in the French woods. Like many children labelled autistic after him, he was mute, order-loving and resistant to social training.

Since then, several figures in history have been labelled retrospectively as possibly having been autistic. These include Einstein – a loner who repeated sentences obsessively until he was seven. He may have suffered from Asperger syndrome, asserts Professor Simon Baron-Cohen, of the Autism Research Centre at Cambridge University. He assessed Einstein and Sir Isaac Newton for classical autistic traits, such as obsessive interests, difficulty in social relationships and problems communicating.

True or not, this kind of analysis does reflect the culture of an almost romantic interest in autism, as some kind of other-worldly state of being that verges on the magical or mystical.

The problem with all this is that the mystique of autism can detract from the very real, down-to-earth sufferings and needs of families living with autism. Parents faced with the lifelong care of a disabled child may want answers as to what caused the disability, but what they will really need to know is how to get through those days that are often impossibly difficult with an intractable child, how to battle public lack of understanding and how to make funds stretch to meet the child's special needs or cover one partner who gives up work to look after their child. They have to live in the very real, nitty-gritty world of getting dressed, brushing teeth and planning the best possible education. All the usual challenges of parenthood can be heartbreakingly difficult for those with autistic children.

The aim of this book is to provide help for families beginning to pick a way through the confusion a diagnosis of autism can cause. It addresses the key issues and points the way to further resources to tackle problems more fully than is possible in these pages.

There is a great deal of material on autism – books, information from support groups, via the Internet and so on. Some of it is extremely useful, some mystifying, some downright unfortunate. Internet material in particular varies from terrific scientific reports to poundingly literal personal accounts, and from obscure, expensive offers of treatment, to long, circumlocutory accounts by people from 'the autism community' giving 'neurotypicals' an insider's account of what it is really like to have autism. This book aims to summarize some of the most current views on and theories about autism in as accessible a way as possible and, by focusing on autism in childhood, provide a starting point for those families embarking on the challenging voyage of discovery that is living with an autistic child.

On this journey, the words of Hans Asperger ('Autistic Psychopathy in Childhood', 1944) remain a source of inspiration and an ideal:

Exceptional human beings must be given exceptional educational treatment, treatment which takes into account their special difficulties. Further, we can show that despite abnormality, human beings can fulfil their social role within the community, especially if they find understanding, love and guidance.

1

Understanding autism

Autism is a complicated neurodevelopmental disorder of social communication that has a profound effect on children's intellectual, social and emotional development. It lasts for life. Autism may be mild or severe, although some people say that this is a meaningless division – that to have autism at all is to be 'other' and you cannot be a little bit autistic. It's something that affects the whole personality – take away the autism, take away the child, say some.

However, autism affects every child differently, so some have higher intellectual functioning, some are better able to function in the community; some will never speak, others are quite articulate; some may have relationships on their own terms, others have profound social difficulties that prove intractable.

The condition, with all its variety, has an organic basis. Autistic disorders are now known to be the result of structural or functional abnormalities in the brain, which probably arise during early brain development while the baby is in the womb. The parts of the brain most commonly affected seem to be those that control attention and are involved in the control and communication of emotion.

The full effects of such brain abnormalities often do not really show until well into toddlerhood, although some parents, either at the time of diagnosis or with hindsight, feel that there was something 'different' about their babies from the start.

Sal was a beautiful elfin baby. 'She seemed to come direct from another world,' said her mother, Frances. 'She had these wonderful blue eyes that seemed to be looking at all sorts of things we mere mortals couldn't see.'

Sal was very good, hardly ever cried, and would spend hours watching her mobile or the scenery moving above her pram. It was only when she was 17 months old that Frances realized that Sal wasn't playing or showing interest in other children. She began to have tantrums, lost the few words she had learned and her interaction with her parents was 'dismal and heartbreaking – we were beside ourselves wondering what we'd done wrong'. Sal had gone, and it took a long time for her parents to accept that she was never going to return.

In effect, this means 'losing' a child – the normal child you thought was yours has gone. It is a heartrending and bewildering transition that may take much time to accomplish. We will return to this very special kind of grief later on (see Chapter 10, Stress and your feelings).

Children as social beings

The main areas of development that you may notice have been affected are social development and communication.

What is social communication? Language is the most obvious element necessary for good communication. By 'language' I mean language in its widest sense, including eye contact, touch, facial expressions, gesture and so on – all the little exchanges that parents and babies typically share well before the first word and the ushering in of speech. Communication involves the entire interaction between people, sharing emotions, games, ideas, TV programmes. Many have noted that the lack of response to others is the area that is most striking in autistic children.

Babies come into the world programmed to respond to social stimuli and form attachments to those who look after them. Much research shows that this bonding process begins at birth and has a lot to do with imitation. Even when still puff-eyed from the rigours of birth, a newborn baby is a keen social observer who immediately listens, recognizes its parents by voice and soon by smell, and watches faces with fascination when fed or cuddled. Some studies have shown that babies will imitate behaviour such as sticking out a tongue within 15 minutes of birth.

This early social sense develops swiftly in the following months – most babies learning many social skills that are vital in helping them interact. For example, joint attention, usually mastered by nine months, is the ability to attend to a toy and a person at the same time, and to share their experience of play with another person, usually an adult. Babies are also adept mindreaders – it is estimated that they see 32,000 examples of facial expressions between three and six months and they learn to monitor the emotional responses of adults, to interpret a look or a tone of voice and react appropriately (for example, crying at a raised voice). They also master social referencing, which is shown by their ability to read a strange

2

situation by looking at their carer's face. For example, if a large dog comes bounding up, a baby may look at its mother to see if it ought to be afraid of the dog or not.

Other basic, hugely important skills involve gestures, such as pointing to things they find interesting to draw other people's attention to them. This is a major developmental step, indicating a sense of self and other.

Skills such as joint attention and social referencing allow children to learn how to behave and respond to life from their nearest and dearest. However, this is where there is a huge divide between typically developing children and autistic children, who may never master these basic developmental skills.

Autistic children seem to lack the innate need to share their experiences that makes a typical child, well into primary school age, shout 'Watch me!' to a parent. Often highly focused on their own activity, autistic children may not imitate others' actions, whereas the typical toddler will copy its mother cleaning, telephoning or a thousand other daily activities.

The typical small child is like a lightning conductor – the instant emotion strikes in another person, any emotion, the child absorbs it at once and often reacts accordingly. It sees joy, humour or anger on its parents' faces as clearly as if they were marked there in bright orange. Autistic children, on the other hand, tend not to look at adults' faces to read the emotional weather forecast there. They tend not to follow others' gaze or pointing gestures or to point at interesting objects themselves.

This lack of social understanding is what distinguishes autism. It means the child may fail to judge correctly everyday situations, emotions and relationships. Not everyone agrees with this. Some see the autistic child as all too socially aware and sensitive, but unable to show it. This inability to see situations from other people's points of view is the single aspect of autism that most impacts their cultural learning and social relationships.

What is autism?

The word 'autism', from the Greek for the 'self', was first used by the psychiatrist Eugen Bleuler in 1911 to describe social withdrawal and detachment in those with schizophrenia.

The word as we understand it today was originally used by Dr Leo Kanner in 1943 to describe a group of young patients, to whom he gave the diagnosis of 'early infantile autism'. These children showed 'autistic' aloneness, mutism (the inability or unwillingness to speak) or very poor language, suspected deafness, a tendency to stare through but not at people, obsessive desire for sameness, use of the third person rather than personal pronouns, echolalia (repeating what you say), literalness, fascination with spinning objects and rhythm, overall serious-mindedness, phenomenal rote memory and many repetitive and stereotypical behaviours. They were often described as being 'in a world of their own'.

This diagnosis formed the basis of today's 'autistic spectrum', which ranges from the severely impaired, who may never achieve independence, to those with above-average IQs and Asperger syndrome – so-called 'high-functioning' autism. For children with a less severe set of symptoms, the description 'pervasive developmental disorders not otherwise specified' (PDDNOS) may be used.

As autism is so complicated and affects each child so differently, it is viewed as a spectrum or 'umbrella' condition in which no two children are the same. For this reason, it is referred to as 'autistic spectrum disorder' (ASD), though, for the purposes of this book, the general terms 'autism' or 'autistic disorder' will be used.

It is classified as a developmental disability, meaning it is a physical disorder, not a psychological one. That is, it is an organic or biological disorder in that it involves some kind of dysfunction of the central nervous system.

Defining autism

Autism is classically defined by the 'triad of impairments' – as delineated by autism expert and consultant psychiatrist Lorna Wing. They are:

- difficulties with speech, language and non-verbal communication
- difficulties with social interaction
- difficulties with imagination and inner language.

Many autistic people also suffer from sensory abnormalities. For example, sounds may be unbearably loud to them or else not heard at all; some children may be abnormally sensitive to touch, and others may hate bright lights. Like other features of autism, this may be due to the way the brain processes sensory information (see Chapter 3, Causes of autism).

Difficulties with speech, language and non-verbal communication
While a small proportion of autistic children never develop speech, most are able to talk. However, the main problem is difficulties with communicating, in using verbal and body language to get in touch with others. Even those with relatively normal language development may find it difficult to start conversations, reply appropriately and volunteer information. For example, a child may be able to repeat perfectly what has been said (echolalia), but cannot use the same words in another situation to request something. The same sort of problem also exists with physical responses (echopraxia).

Difficulties with social interaction
Those with autism often have difficulties starting and maintaining relationships with their peers, though it may be that they relate better to parents, carers and other adults who are able to anticipate their needs and read their emotions. As other children do not have this ability, the autistic child struggles to interact with his peers. It is not that autistic children cannot make friends, it is just that, often, they do not know how to. Teaching an autistic child social skills is critical to their development. People with autism also tend to have problems with understanding how other people are feeling or interpreting facial expressions.

Difficulties with imagination and inner language
Imaginary or 'pretend' play, such as playing babies with dolls or driving with a chair, is something we take for granted as part of a child's growing up. It is also a very important part of a child's development. However, children with autism tend not to play in this way at all.

Sensory problems

Babies usually experience 'cross-modal transfer' or 'cross-modal matching' when they put objects into their mouths at around four months old. 'Cross-modal transfer' or 'cross-modal matching' is the process whereby the senses of touch, smell, sight and taste work together to help the baby learn about objects.

In children with autism, there is evidence that this process is impaired. Thus, sensory integration problems are common and may well account for many apparent behaviour problems. Sensory problems may be due to abnormalities in the cerebellum, which helps control our responses to sensory stimuli. Difficulties include an acute dislike of touch or of certain textures; hatred of certain sounds, such as hairdryers or microwaves, or overly loud noises; and extreme dislike of certain foods or textures of foods.

How common is autism – is it on the rise?

There have been several reports of a sharp rise in autism, along with much dispute as to whether or not this is a 'real' rise or due to better understanding and diagnosis of autism. Some argue that autism is increasing because of environmental factors, such as allergies and sensitivity to vaccines, genetic factors or a mixture of all these. Others argue that autism is now recognized in those with other disorders, such as tuberous sclerosis and Down's syndrome, which automatically increases the total number of those with autism. As a result, the figures vary – some say that autism affects 1 in 1000 people, while others put it as high as 1 in 110.

For example, California researchers say that autism cases increased six-fold in the past 15 years and doubled in the past 4 years (1998–2002) and that even this rise might be an underestimate. An earlier Californian study pinpointed a 273 per cent increase in the number of autistic children entering state treatment centres between 1987 and 1998. However, the researchers at the University of California, Davis' MIND Institute were unable to say why.

In the UK, which has a less rigorous method of diagnosing autism cases than California, figures for 2003 indicate that 500,000 people in the UK have autism, including Asperger syndrome. Of these, 100,000 are children. In 10 years, the incidence has almost doubled to 91 per 10,000 people – nearly 1 per cent of the population. One study of GP records in the UK by James Kaye, of Boston University, found that diagnoses of autism increased seven-fold between 1988 and 1999. There is speculation that an environmental factor is to blame, though the researchers at Boston ruled out any link with the MMR vaccine (see Chapter 3, Causes of autism).

In America as a whole, figures indicate that 2 to 6 per 1000 individuals have autism (Centers for Disease Control and Prevention, 2001). This means that as many as 1.5 million Americans today are believed to have some form of autism. According to figures from the US Department of Education, autism is growing at a rate of 10–17 per cent per year – an estimated 4 million Americans in the next decade.

According to the Autism Council of Australia, the number of children diagnosed has doubled, from 1 in 1000 to 1 in 500. Some regions, such as Geelong in Victoria, have recorded rates as high as 1 in 200.

It's generally agreed that severe 'core' autism only affects about 4 in every 10,000 people, while 50–60 in every 10,000 are affected by some disorder from the autistic spectrum.

Whether there has been a real increase or it is being more readily diagnosed, the end result is the same. According to American autism expert Dr Marie Bristol Power of the National Institute of Child Health and Human Development, Bethesda, Maryland, it is a 'pressing public health problem' that demands provision to be made as a matter of urgency.

Why is autism more common in boys?

Autism is four times more common in boys than girls, and Asperger syndrome is ten times more common in boys. The reason is believed to be genetic. The theory is that it may be associated with variations in genes on the X chromosome. Boys only have one X chromosome, whereas girls have two. This means that if a gene on a boys' only X chromosome doesn't work properly, he doesn't have an extra copy, as girls do, to compensate in times of need. Organically, males tend to be more susceptible overall to damage than girls, whether through hereditary disease, acquired infection or other conditions. As it is now accepted that autism has an organic cause, the naturally greater vulnerability of males may well account for there being more boys with autism than girls.

Hans Asperger held the view that autism and Asperger syndrome are at the extreme end of a spectrum of behaviour normally associated with 'maleness' – attention to detail and single-mindedness, for example. Other exaggerated 'male' features include insistence on identical routines, obsessional interests, preoccupation with certain objects as well as superior visual and spatial skills. One has to remember that Asperger (like his fellow Viennese, Freud) was working in the 1940s and probably had a very traditional view of typical male (and female) behaviour. That is, that men were typically more interested in details, machinery and objects and how they work, while placing less importance on social interactions, and women were more reliant on social intelligence and contact and less interested and able when it came to mechanical things, such as fixing the car! There is a whole body of research into this interesting cultural heritage, specifically the link between autism and professions such as engineering, classically a male profession with less reliance on social intelligence than other professions. Professor Simon Baron-Cohen of Cambridge University conducted a survey of the fathers and grandfathers of people with autism and found that they were twice as likely to be engineers than the relatives of non-autistic people. A further study at Cambridge University found that students of science were six times more likely than students of the humanities to have autistic relatives.

However, Professor Christopher Gillberg, Professor of Psychiatry at the University of Gothenburg, believes that the prevalence of Asperger syndrome in boys may simply be exaggerated as girls' social and communications skills are generally better developed than those of boys. For example, girls are often diagnosed with an unspecified learning disorder or perceptual problem, while their social and communication deficits may go unrecognized. Hence, symptoms in girls may not be recognized as autistic.

The prognosis?

While autism is generally spoken of as being lifelong, no one can really say clearly what the outcome of your child will be. There are too many stories of children, written off by the medical profession early in life, who went on to transcend their difficulties in a spectacular way. Temple Grandin, the famous autistic animal science professor at Colorado State University, speculates that she might now be 'rotting in front of a TV somewhere' if a teacher had not channelled her obsessive interest in cattle chutes into what became an international career in designing livestock-handling facilities. While she remains autistic, with certain communicative and sensory differences, she, like others with autism, has carved out a path that capitalizes on her strengths.

The eyes don't have it
A study by Dr Ami Klin, Professor of Child Psychology and Psychiatry at Yale University, explored the nature of the autistic person's inability to understand and communicate with other people.

The research found that autistic people focus twice as much attention on the mouths and bodies of people as on their eyes during social situations. This means that they may miss important feelings and non-verbal clues coming via the eyes, such as irony or humour, because they are so focused on the words coming out of the mouth.

However, this may be as a result of a coping mechanism, according to Dr Klin – perhaps even the autistic person's best bet for picking up meaning. The study also suggested that, even when those with autism do look at the eyes, they don't gain much information from them. The more autistic people looked at the mouths, the more socially competent they were in real life. This is the opposite of normal social expectations, which would be that the more they focused on the eyes, the more competent they would be.

The study also showed that those with autism who focused more on objects were more likely to suffer from social problems, suggesting that they were not focusing on the people at all and so missing even more cues – both verbal and non-verbal.

The study also raises the possibility that eye tracking devices could be used as an early detection tool for autism.

The future depends very much on the individual nature of your child. Her IQ is one important factor. Another is how marked her social and communication difficulties are early on, as the better those skills, the better the likely eventual outcome. You may gain some idea of the future by how well your child progresses in the year after diagnosis, especially if the diagnosis is made early.

Perhaps most important of all is early intervention, which aims to change behaviour and improve speech.

The key point is help. Getting in early, with sustained, sensitive help, can make an enormous difference to your child. Some parents are told that their child has severe learning difficulties as well as autism. This may not be true – they do have difficulty learning, but this is because they are autistic, not because they have a lower intelligence. This is where parents are in a position to make a difference, to find ways round that difficulty and access the intelligence within. Autism is treatable and, with the correct input, children can make huge strides. It is natural to hope for normal development, but many parents, looking back over the years, find that their child has progressed far beyond their initial expectations and can take more pride in that than they ever anticipated.

As parents, you are the expert on your child. That puts you in a privileged position from which to start giving your child the help she needs to blossom, even though others will probably be involved at some point. (More on types of help and therapy in Chapters 5 and 6.)

2

The autistic spectrum

Traditionally, there are two main 'types' of autism – autism and Asperger syndrome. Common to both are symptoms such as rigid, repetitive behaviour, resistance to change and a lack of imagination. Asperger children are usually viewed as abler, better at language (though they may sound strangely formal or stilted) and with average or above-average intelligence.

The ongoing argument about whether autism and Asperger syndrome are the same or different conditions may well turn out to be irrelevant. Research is still catching up with the pioneering work done by Kanner and Asperger in the 1940s, which was initially overshadowed by the Second World War and Freud. Today, it is speculated that the autistic spectrum, or range of autistic disorders, is much more subtle than this and potentially involves a much greater variety of disorders than at first thought. Colwyn Trevarthen, Professor of Psychology at the University of Edinburgh, has concluded that autism and Asperger syndrome are better viewed as differing in the level of impairment experienced on a continuing spectrum of severity rather than as two separate conditions.

Bear in mind also that autism may only be part of the picture for many, who may display its features as part of a range of difficulties, including mental retardation and seizure disorders. In addition, the condition may evolve and change with time and development, depending on the individual child.

All this means that no two children with autism are alike. At one end of the spectrum, a child may never speak and be able to do little for himself; another child, diagnosed with Asperger syndrome, may be articulate, intelligent and go on to university, have a career and sustain a marriage, yet remain marked out by the social aloofness for which autism is famous.

Definitions of 'types' of autism now include 'loners', who may be very bright Asperger syndrome sufferers, and 'active but odd' – Dr Wing's shorthand for Asperger syndrome, used to differentiate it from the classic self-absorption of autism, but is now a phrase that seems to have taken on a life of its own as a definition for abler autistic individuals.

11

Where do you draw the line? Many people have some autistic traits, such as enjoyment of their own company and eccentric hobbies they do alone. (Indeed, one writer described the UK as an appropriate abode for autistic people as such traits align well with the traditional British eccentric!)

It may be helpful to think of the condition as a disorder of empathy. The central ability that seems to be lacking is an understanding of what others think and feel – what psychologists call a theory of mind. However, there are intriguing hints from the hinterlands of autism that even this is not as simple as first thought, that autistic children may have their own understanding of others. Certainly, according to many parents, they don't miss much of what is going on around them.

Kanner's autism and Asperger syndrome

While the distinction between these conditions may be a false one, the separate terms are still in common use.

Kanner's autism, or, childhood autism

In 1943, Dr Leo Kanner produced the first description of a group of autistic patients. The traits he noted included:

- withdrawal and aloneness
- mutism or language that fails to convey meaning
- delayed developmental milestones
- phenomenal rote memory
- echolalia
- concrete thinking
- reference to self in the third person
- obsessive desire for sameness
- good relationships with objects, but not with people
- fascination with spinning objects and rhythm
- staring through people rather than at them
- anxiety in the presence of others.

Asperger syndrome

First described by Hans Asperger in 1944, it is often viewed as the upper end of the spectrum and is sometimes called high-functioning autism. It was not until 1994, though, that Asperger syndrome became an acknowledged clinical diagnosis.

Asperger syndrome is often differentiated from autism by the fact that children with the syndrome may be much more articulate than those who have classic autism, but still lack social nous and communication skills.

They may have rigid routines and rituals (or 'stereotypical' behaviour). They may have a very high IQ and, though viewed as odd or eccentric, find a place in society and compensate for any lack of social skills with their memory or excellent academic abilities.

Clumsiness is another distinguishing feature.

Many of those diagnosed with Asperger syndrome have phenomenal memories and may focus on one or two areas of special interest, such as train schedules or historical facts. A child's overall language may be limited, but, in the area of special expertise, it may be scholarly, though pedantic, with little flexibility and real grasp of the meaning of the words, giving the impression that these 'little professors', as Asperger called them, are using rote memory rather than making spontaneous observations on the subject.

The child may be socially aware, but, sadly, aware of his own social limitations and interact in an inappropriate way. Even the most able may lack common sense.

Most recent studies show that the only differences between the conditions lie in the level of IQ and general ability to do things for themselves – both being greater in those with Asperger syndrome.

The heart of autism

A core feature of autism is that those with this condition do not understand how other people perceive their behaviour, facial expressions, tone of voice and communication in general. They also have difficulties with expressing their own emotions in an appropriate way and sharing emotions and interests.

Jack would run on his tiptoes across a room and flap his hands at intervals. He generally ignored people at the expense of watching the washing machine. He was quite happy watching it work and could read the manual perfectly.

His mother Sammie tried to get his social life going by inviting little friends round to play. The height of Jack's interaction was trying to interest his friend in his own passion. Sammie saw with horror that Jack had absolutely no idea how very uninteresting this was to most other little boys after about two minutes. He would continue to sit in front of the machine long after his little companion had gone into the front room to explore the toy box.

The story varies from child to child, but the core elements are the same: their inability to understand how they may affect others and register how others may perceive what they do, say or express with their body language and facial expressions, as well as their inability to perceive what others are expressing with their words and body language.

This, though, doesn't necessarily mean that children with autism feel no affection (a common myth about autism). On the contrary, they may have even more of a need for their parents than normal. While they may not be able to express it now, with time and training, many children do learn to show their love of and need for their families.

Is my child autistic?

Many children with an autistic disorder first come to their doctor because of a language delay. While some children never speak, a typical pattern is for children to lose the few words that they have already learned, maybe at around 18 months of age.

One of the hardest aspects of autism is its diagnosis in a child previously believed to be 'normal'. If children don't display any autistic traits until perhaps they are three or four years old and then 'change', the possibility of autism comes as a shock, which can cause prolonged grieving (see Chapter 10, Stress and your feelings).

Many parents, especially first-time ones, do not notice any difficulties, though some may have a vague notion that all is not as expected or may notice that their child is different. For example, he resists cuddles or has unusual eye contact, even if he doesn't miss a thing of what's going on around him.

Stephan's parents were acutely concerned when, at two and a half, he developed unusual behaviour habits. They thought that he had maybe had a virus and was suffering some form of post-viral syndrome. He had always been rather a quiet child, but now he seemed to drift into his own world and sit quietly for periods of time. At first, his parents would put a cassette on for him, assuming that he was winding down after playgroup or other activities.

Then the playgroup leader contacted them. She was concerned, too, and strongly urged a doctor's appraisal. She said that, at playgroup, Stephan was increasingly ignoring the other children and acting deaf – for example, taking no notice when called for group activities, yet running up at once when hearing the slightest sound of something he liked, such as a favourite song. He was also very 'obstinate' about his play activities and insisted on monopolizing small toys, such as model animals, which he could line up in rows.

Joe did not speak until he was three, and then he would echo what his parents and others said to him. For example, if someone asked, 'How's Joe today?' he would reply, 'How's Joe today?' He also developed terrible tantrums, which his increasingly uneasy parents hoped might be delayed 'terrible twos'. During these outbursts, Joe would flap his hands – a mannerism that gradually spread into his other behaviour until he would do it when even the slightest bit agitated about something.

Joe also showed signs of hyperactivity and was increasingly distractible; his mother had to keep him in reins when shopping because he would shoot off at the slightest chance and be quite hard to catch again. On questioning at the doctor's, his parents said that Joe had always struck them as normal, though his mother did mention that, when picked up, even from babyhood, Joe had never snuggled into her or offered any help – he was like an 'ironing board'.

The triad of impairments – of social interaction, communication and imagination – forms the basis of a diagnosis of autism (see Chapter 4, Diagnosis). A diagnosis is best made by a specialist, but typical things to look out for are the following.

- If your child is late starting to speak and doesn't use gestures beforehand. Any speech that does come may be repetitive, dull or idiosyncratic. He may confuse 'you' and 'I' and refer to himself in the third person.
- Your child won't or can't seem to fix his gaze on you.
- He doesn't share with you – for example, he doesn't show, bring or point out objects of interest and enjoyment.
- If he becomes increasingly remote from, and unresponsive to, you and the family.
- He seems generally aloof, does not form friendships and prefers playing alone.
- If your child shows a lack of make-believe play and role play – for example, he doesn't play games where he imitates people's

social roles, such as mummies and daddies, schools, doctors, postman and so on.

- He seems indifferent to the feelings of others – for example, if you hurt yourself, he doesn't react.
- If he is also indifferent to social conventions.
- He is routine-bound and strongly resists change.
- If your child has obsessive rituals and perhaps screams if prevented from carrying them out.
- He may also have sudden screaming fits that you can't always see a reason for or laugh or show other mood swings that, again, aren't always understandable.
- Your child has obsessions about particular types of items and may collect them to the exclusion of many other activities – the search for 'sterile sameness'.
- If he has odd, repetitive movements, such as hand flapping, twisting, rocking, walking on tiptoe.
- He is hyperactive.
- If your child shows behaviour problems, such as set-in-stone fads about drinking, eating and sleeping.
- He shows acute sensitivity to certain sensory stimuli, such as touch, light, noise and so on. A classic autism pose is to sit with his hands over his ears or be under- or oversensitive to pain or else hate being touched.
- If he has impressive special skills, such as early reading ('islets of competence', see Savant syndrome below).

None of the above necessarily means that your child has autism. For example, many boys learn to speak later than girls, many toddlers become fascinated by specific subjects (fire engines, Barbie dolls), many children go through food fads and are hard to get to bed and learning to read early can happen just because the child is bright! The real question is whether or not you as parents are happy. Sometimes parents just have an intuitive feeling that something is not quite right with their child and this feeling should never be ignored.

Savant syndrome

This is a rare condition in which the child has areas ('islets') of outstanding competence in certain subjects, such as the artist Steven Wiltshire – famous for his ability to glance at a building and draw it from memory.

There are five main general areas of savant expertise, according to Professor Darold Treffert, of St Agnes Hospital, Fond du Lac, Wisconsin, an expert in the savant field. These are music, art, lightning calculating or other mathematical skills, calendar calculating and mechanical or spatial skills. Music is the most common savant talent, followed by art and then, less commonly, mechanical ability. All these skills are linked with a special type of extraordinary memory that can retain a multitude of details in a highly specialized area, such as memorizing the UK motorway system.

Calendar calculating, for example – very rare in the general population – is the ability to name the day of the week that a date will occur on in any particular year. The so-called 'calculating twins', reported extensively in neurological literature (including Oliver Sacks's *The Man Who Mistook His Wife for a Hat*), have a calendar calculating span of over 40,000 years, going backwards or forwards in time. They can also remember the weather for every day of their adult life.

Other skills reported, though less often, include languages, highly developed sensory discrimination in smell or touch, perfect knowledge of time without a clock or watch or outstanding knowledge in specific fields, such as statistics, history or navigation. There have also been some reports of extrasensory perception skills in savants.

A 'prodigious savant' is a very rare case of someone who has a special skill or ability that is so outstanding that it would be spectacular even if it were to occur in a typical person. According to Professor Treffert, there are probably fewer than 50 prodigious savants worldwide.

What causes Savant syndrome?

For centuries, the phenomenon was shrugged off with the term 'idiot savant'. Now, modern neurology is beginning to find clues as to why some people have these apparently inexplicable flashes of genius.

One theory is that, in cases where the left part of the brain has sustained injury, the right hemisphere compensates. The skills most often seen in savants are those associated with the right hemisphere and those most lacking are those associated with the left hemisphere.

Because of the brain injury, savants come to rely on more primitive memory circuits of procedural or habit memory, rather than the higher-level ones of semantic or declarative memory. It is thought that this combination of right-brain skills and procedural memory results in the extraordinary abilities of savants.

An estimated 10 per cent of those with autism have savant skills – and just 1 per cent of the non-autistic population, including those with mental retardation, which is less than 1 per cent of the whole population. This said, primitive memory and right-brain capacity still exist in us all. So, is it possible to tap into and use these dormant capabilities and display savant abilities ourselves?

This question has been posed by Professor Treffert, who speculates that there may be a savant within everyone. For example, people who have sustained brain injury sometimes gain savant skills when they recover; the same applies to elderly people with certain degenerative brain conditions. Whatever the case may be, there is a wealth of literature on this fascinating subject (see the Further reading and Useful addresses sections at the back of the book), but neurologists still have a long way to go before the syndrome, like all autistic disorders, is fully explained. As Professor Treffert puts it, 'The significance of the savant syndrome lies in our inability to explain it. The savants stand as a clear reminder of our ignorance about ourselves, especially how our brains function.'

Impaired or different?

Writing in the *Guardian* about her two autistic sons and their sensory difficulties, Charlotte Moore has stated that, 'we still assess an autistic child in terms of educational handicap, and fail to recognize him as the differently-wired being he really is'.

Just how differently autistic people are wired has been explored by researcher Andrew Walker, of Birmingham University, who has Asperger syndrome. Dr Walker explores the hypothesis that we live in a bipolar society, made up of people descended from two different strains of early man, and that autistic people actually evolved separately because of different environmental conditions.

According to this idea, autistic and 'normal' people are descended from two different races – Neanderthals (Homo sapiens neanderthalensis) and Cro-Magnons (Homo sapiens sapiens). Cro-Magnons flourished and developed higher-level social skills because of the more favourable southerly climate, while the harsher, more northerly latitudes caused a greater dependency on technology and lower population levels among the Neanderthals.

Thus, autism may be a genetic trait with a racial basis. The theory is that autistic people (presumably descended from Neanderthals) have a racially inherited inability to perceive and communicate 'memes', or, ideas pertaining to social communication. A meme (pronounced meem) is, roughly, a unit of social and cultural information passed on between members of the same species, rather like the way in which genes are passed on biologically.

Autistic people cannot communicate in this way because, perceiving the universe in terms of the strictly physical, memes are 'cognitively invisible' to them. The result is two groups of people who each have an apparently separate reality and few common terms of reference.

This inheritance theory might also explain why society has an either/or tendency regarding arts and science. Thus, people tend to become either artists or doctors and place their trust in either technology or more spiritual guides.

Elegant or contrived? However tongue in cheek this theory might be, it is an eloquent metaphor for the difference of autism, for the alienation felt by those with autism in our society and the consequent, often impossible, pressure to 'normalize' the autistic. Dr Walker suggests that, instead of perceiving autistic people (he also likens their plight to that of the Australian aborigines, who have for so long been viewed as different and therefore in need of social correction) as disordered and in need of a cure, they could be regarded more properly as 'differently functioning'.

3

Causes of autism

What is the cause of autism? This is one medical mystery many parents want the solution to. The possible answers suggested so far are bewildering in their range and complexity. Take the rampant media coverage of the MMR (combined measles, mumps and rubella) vaccine as a cause of autism; then the further claims that the cause is linked with digestive problems, such as lack of secretin and/ or intolerance of wheat and milk. How can autism have so many different possible causes and if, instead, it is one, which is correct?

There is an understandable urge to find a clear answer when something goes wrong, when parental expectations are devastated and no one can explain why. It is equally understandable that some parents want government support and funding to help them manage the burden of caring for a disabled child. A clearly proven cause would pave the way, if there were to be a proven legal liability.

The truth, as yet, is not that simple. This complicated neurological disorder is likely to prove multifactorial, though the leading candidate would appear to be genetic inheritance. Meanwhile, the Medical Research Council in the UK is funding one of the largest studies of autism ever attempted. Chaired by Professor Andrew Hall of the London School of Hygiene and Tropical Medicine, the study will attempt to find out what causes the condition and study any possible link with the MMR vaccine. It will examine a representative sample of health records from two million people, drawn from 300 general practices across the UK.

The genetic factor

The causes of autism are most likely to be genetic. I use the word 'causes', not 'cause', as a complicated blend of genes is probably involved. 'Autism', as we have seen, is a general term for a spectrum condition, so it is likely to be caused by a combination of several different genetic abnormalities and neurological mechanisms. For example, it is thought that certain children are born with irregular segments of genetic code that makes them susceptible to autism.

Other researchers are looking at the possibility that unstable genes may interfere with brain development, again resulting in autism.

At which stage of development this takes place isn't known, but researchers suspect it takes place while the developing baby is still in the womb. For example, Frank De Stephano and Robert Chen of the US Center for Infectious Disease Control and Prevention note that autism has a strong genetic component and that the associated defects probably occur prior to birth, even though the effects may only become apparent later.

While people may have a genetic vulnerability to autism, inherited factors themselves may not always be enough to explain its development. Some experts believe that there is also an environmental trigger or triggers that might have more of an impact on a susceptible person than on someone else. Again, it is by no means clear what the triggers are, but research is ongoing into several possible culprits, such as exposure to chemicals. For example, scientists at the University of California at Berkeley are conducting a study that will test the tissues of both autistic and non-autistic children for residues of heavy metals, such as benzene and mercury. The premise is that some children may be genetically more susceptible than others to damage by these agents.

The evidence for a genetic cause

There is a lot of evidence that autism runs in families. Many families seem to have a pattern of autism or related disabilities. According to Dr Wendy Kates of Johns Hopkins School of Medicine in Baltimore, USA, approximately half of all close relatives of autistic children have milder symptoms of autism.

Studies of identical twins (who clearly share identical genetic material) and non-identical twins (sharing half their brother's or sister's genes) have shown that autism is more common in identical than non-identical twins. This shows a clear genetic link, though there are cases where one twin has autism and the other doesn't.

Siblings of those with autism have a higher than average chance of developing autism themselves, which also reinforces the genetic link to the disorder. Likewise, some families have a member such as a grandfather or an uncle renowned for his odd behaviour, often accepted in family legend as 'eccentricity'.

Further evidence for the genetic factor is that autism tends to occur more often in those who have certain medical conditions with

21

a known genetic basis. Between 5 and 10 per cent of those with autism have an identifiable chromosomal abnormality. Such conditions include 'fragile X syndrome' – one of the most commonly identified causes of autism (though a relatively rare condition). Found only in boys, it is characterized by learning difficulties and an unusual facial appearance with large ears, long nose and high forehead. Another condition is tuberous sclerosis, a syndrome that causes seizures, mental disorders and nodules or tumours to form on the brain.

Further evidence for the genetic theory is that boys are affected four times more often than girls, which is believed to be linked with the fact that boys have only one X chromosome (see Chapter 1).

Is autism two conditions?

A major study in London has found that autism may be a combination of two separate conditions, each controlled by different sets of genes.

Professor Robert Plomin of the Institute of Psychiatry in London and Dr Angelica Ronald, also of the Institute, studied 4000 pairs of twins.

They identified two sets of symptoms, each associated with two completely different sets of genes – the social and the non-social.

The social component is autistic children's communication difficulties and their failure to understand that other people have minds of their own. The non-social aspect is children's obsessional interest in objects and factual details.

Autism may be the result when a child inherits extreme versions of both sets of genes governing the social and non-social aspects of autism, the researchers suggest.

If autism is indeed two conditions, it goes some way towards explaining why researchers have found it difficult to isolate one gene as being responsible for the disorder.

'Computer geek' genes?
Doctors at the MIND Institute in Sacramento, California, think high rates of autism in the Silicon Valley area could be down to the 'computer geek' genes of its workers. The study suggests that 'computer geek' men probably find it difficult to mix socially and so are more likely to meet partners who also carry autistic genes than the rest of the population.

The number of autistic children attending treatment centres in California between 1987 and 1998 rose by 273 per cent – a much higher percentage than the rest of the US. However, this theory doesn't explain the cluster of cases found in predominantly blue-collar areas.

Autism and the brain

As far back as 1964, Dr Bernard Rimland, an internationally recognized authority on autism and director of the Autism Research Institute, San Diego, California, USA, provided evidence that established autism as a biological disorder, not a psychological one. Since then, several studies have found differences between typical and autistic brains. As we have seen, autistic disorders have been clearly linked with structural or functional abnormalities in the brain that probably occur early on in the baby's development in the womb. Neurons in these regions appear smaller than normal and have stunted nerve fibres, which may interfere with nerve signalling.

Whether this happens spontaneously or other causes are implicated has yet to be established. Researchers are exploring whether certain conditions, such as the mother's health during pregnancy, problems during delivery or other factors may interfere with normal brain development. Some Dutch evidence suggested that excessive consumption of alcohol during pregnancy caused autism in babies, but this was a small study and its results were not viewed as conclusive (though there is no doubt that drinking too much in pregnancy does have adverse effects on the baby). Still other researchers are investigating the effects of problems during pregnancy or delivery, as well as environmental factors, such as viral infections, metabolic imbalances and exposure to environmental chemicals. For example, researchers at the Cambridge Autism Research Centre are investigating the possibility that excess amounts of the male hormone testosterone in the womb may adversely affect the development of social skills.

Drugs taken by some pregnant women are also coming under scrutiny. At the University of Rochester, USA, a study is focusing on how certain teratogens (substances that cause birth defects) could lead to autism. The researchers are looking at the impact of the teratogens on a gene called hoxa1, which is supposed to appear briefly only in the first trimester of pregnancy and is linked with the development of the brainstem. Well-proven viral infections linked with autism include rubella, which may damage the unborn baby's brain if the mother contracts it in the first three months of pregnancy, causing several problems including autism. However, in many countries vaccination programmes have made this much rarer.

Neuronal abnormalities vary from person to person and are not found in all people with autism, but, so far, some of the areas highlighted include:

- the frontal lobes – responsible for planning, solving problems, understanding the behaviour of others and impulse control
- the limbic system – including the amygdala and hippocampus, which are responsible for the regulation of emotions – for example, recognizing emotions, reading people's facial expressions and guessing what they may be feeling – the hippocampus also being involved in recalling recent experiences and new information; animal experiments show that removal of the amygdala and hippocampus results in autistic behaviour
- the cerebellum, which is in the back and lower part of the brain and governs motor coordination, balance and the muscles used in speaking, as well as the process of shifting attention between auditory and visual stimuli
- the parietal areas, which control hearing, speech and language
- the corpus callosum, which passes information from one side of the brain to the other.

For example, Wendy Kates and her colleagues at Johns Hopkins School of Medicine in Baltimore, USA, used magnetic resonance imaging (MRI) to look at the brains of seven-year-old identical twins. One of the boys had classical autism, while his twin had only some of the symptoms of autism, including language and social problems. When the researchers compared the brain scans of the two boys, they found several differences.

The amygdala – the area involved in emotion – and the hippocampus – important for learning and memory – in the autistic child were about half the size of these parts of his twin brother's brain. The cerebellum and the caudate nucleus – thought to be involved in shifting attention from one task to another – were also significantly smaller.

The link with neurological differences is further backed up by the fact that those with autism are more likely than others to have seizures. Indeed, around a third of children with autism have seizures.

The studies were done using the brain-scanning techniques of computer axial tomography (CAT) scans and MRI. The shortcomings of these are that, in some cases, anomalies in the brain may be too subtle to be picked up by current scanning techniques. However, as the technology becomes more sophisticated, it is likely that it will be possible to pick up increasingly minute structural differences.

Other studies suggest that people with autism have differences in certain neurotransmitters, the chemical messengers of the nervous system. For example, high levels of the neurotransmitter serotonin have been found in a number of people with autism. As neurotransmitters are responsible for passing along nerve impulses in the brain and nervous system, it is possible that they arc involved in the sensory abnormalities that are often a feature of autism.

At the National Institute of Mental Health (NIMH) in Bethesda, Maryland, researchers have used MRI to identify which parts of the brain are energized during specific mental tasks. In a study of teenage boys with autism, the scans showed less brain activity during problem-solving and language tasks than was the case among those in the control group. The autistic teenagers were also less successful at the tasks than their peers without autism. In a study of younger children, researchers observed low levels of activity in the parietal areas and the corpus callosum.

Such research may help scientists determine whether autism is a problem with specific areas of the brain or the transmission of signals from one part of the brain to another.

Autistic children have larger brains

Evidence that the basic brain systems are disrupted in autistic children comes from several studies. Research at the University of California indicates that autistic children have brains that are large for their age. It appears that they have abnormally fast brain growth, which begins around four months of age, according to Professor Eric Courchesne, who used magnetic resonance imaging to measure the excessive brain development.

In practical terms, the discovery could revolutionize diagnosis of autism and treatment as paediatricians or parents could simply measure the head circumference of newborns and babies during their first year, looking out for any sudden unusual jump in size that might be an early warning sign of autism. Professor Courchesne's study showed that the brain of a one-year-old autistic child was the size of that of a typical two-year-old, while a two- to four-year-old autistic child had a brain the size of a normal 10- to 12-year-old's. The trigger for the unusual growth is not yet known.

Another study by Dr Geraldine Dawson, Professor of Psychology at the University of Washington, showed that children with autism registered no difference in brain activity when shown pictures of a neutral face and a fearful face. Normally, babies show different reactions to a fearful face than to a neutral one by seven months. The response is believed to be a survival one, built in by evolution, and lack of it suggests that autistic children do not interpret or respond to emotional cues at a fundamental level.

A further study by Dr Dawson found that autistic three- and four-year-olds responded to pictures of familiar toys, but not to photographs of their mothers. Again, a very basic brain process – the recognition of the child's nearest and dearest – was disrupted. Like the test for larger brains, the differences in the brain activity of autistic children and normally developing ones could prove the basis for earlier diagnosis.

26

Vaccines

Led by a narrow, sensationalist media obsessed with the thorny question of a relationship between vaccines and autism, this subject continues to be hotly debated. Study after study has refuted the link between vaccines and autism, but the anti-vaccine lobby is adamant that there is a link.

The original research at the Royal Free Hospital by Dr Andrew Wakefield in 1988 (who has since left the Royal Free) was carried out with just 12 children.

As noted above, several large-scale reports from around the world have failed to find a link between autism and one major suspect – the combined measles, mumps and rubella (MMR) vaccine, given to children around the age of 18 months. The question is further complicated by the fact that autistic differences that had previously been dormant often start showing at around the same age as the vaccine is given, but are unrelated to it. If autism is diagnosed at this age, there is certainly no reason for parents to feel guilty that they have somehow caused it by letting their child be given the MMR vaccine as the two events are simply coincidental.

A study by the UK's Medical Research Council (MRC) concluded that there is no evidence to suggest a causal link between the MMR vaccine and autism. The American journal *Paediatrics* even stated that a child's immune system could cope with 10,000 vaccines at one time if it had to.

The consensus seems to be that the majority of medical evidence is against vaccines causing autism, though there may be a possibility that the vaccine contributes to the disorder in a small number of vulnerable children.

Despite all this evidence, thousands of families in the UK believe that their child regressed developmentally and became autistic after having the MMR vaccine. The figures show an ongoing loss of confidence in doctors and the government on the part of parents. Some parents may also feel that compensation is more likely to be won if a cause can be proved.

The 93 per cent uptake of MMR in the early 1990s was close enough to the World Health Organization's target of 95 per cent to keep the risk of measles at bay. However, statistics from the Public Health Laboratory Service, published in 2002, show that just 70 per cent of 16-month-old children received the MMR vaccine in March

– a drop of 6 per cent since the end of 2001 and well below the government's target of 95 per cent. This makes the return of measles more likely. Globally, measles is still a major childhood killer, with more than 30 million cases and nearly 900,000 deaths a year.

MMR – has the media misled the public?

Media stories about the safety of the MMR vaccine have left people with the wrong impression that scientists are evenly divided as to whether or not the vaccine is linked with the occurrence of autism, according to a survey at Cardiff University, Wales. In fact, the vast majority of doctors and scientists believe firmly in the safety of the MMR, but 53 per cent of British people questioned wrongly said that there was equal evidence on both sides of the debate owing to media coverage that gave space to both sides of the debate, according to Professor Justin Lewis and his colleagues. Only 23 per cent of the public realized that the bulk of evidence was in favour of the vaccine.

The researchers also asked whether or not journalists ought to subject the claims of 'maverick' scientists such as Wakefield to closer scrutiny before reporting them. Half of the British public agreed – 48 per cent felt that, if a scientist makes minority claims, the media should wait until the findings are confirmed before reporting them.

On the other hand, 34 per cent felt that research such as Wakefield's should be given coverage because it is 'news'.

The research raised implications for the debate about fairness in journalism, and suggested that legal definitions of impartiality in broadcast journalism should not be interpreted in a simplistic fashion.

Professor Lewis concluded that, while Wakefield's claims may be of legitimate public interest, the report showed that caution from journalists and scientists was key when research questioned the safety of something that is widely used – especially an issue where any decline in confidence could have serious consequences for public health.

Some researchers claim that the mercury in some vaccines given to babies may be a contributory cause of autism. One study in the USA found that children who had been given such vaccines were more than twice as likely to develop autism than children who had not had them. However, other doctors say that the toxic effects of mercury have been studied and autism is not among them.

Mercury is not used in the MMR. In the UK, the only mercury-containing vaccine given routinely to all children is the DTP (diphtheria, tetanus and polio) vaccine and this is being phased out.

4

Diagnosis

Jack seemed to be a normal baby but his parents became concerned in toddlerhood when he seemed increasingly to be 'in his own world' and able to tune his parents out. He showed no interest in other children or pretend play. His favourite activity was to put all his toys into several shoeboxes that he would line up by his bed. His posture and body movements struck his parents as odd – when he should have been learning to run and jump, he seemed to lurch and move at an odd angle. His father was disappointed when Jack showed no interest in playing football with him.

Jack also developed an acute sensitivity to noise that was highly disruptive. 'He'd react very badly to mechanical noises – the TV, the Hoover, washing machine,' says his mother. 'They really seemed to distress him and he'd run away and sit by his bed with his hands over his ears. My parents thought it was just a phase and told us Jack would grow out of it. We thought he was having hearing problems and took him to the doctor. It took us a further three years to get a diagnosis, and we had to insist every inch of the way, with doctors, health visitors, social workers. We were dismissed as fussy parents.'

Confusion among professionals is one of the commonest sources of distress to parents of children with autism. Statistics suggest that only about 10 per cent of children with autistic disorders are diagnosed following the parents initially saying to professionals that something is wrong with their child. In the USA, the average age of diagnosis is between two and three years; in the UK, it may not be until school age or later. Getting a diagnosis of autism all too often involves a long, bumpy journey from doctor to doctor, until at last one of them finally pronounces the verdict. However, there are reasons for this – diagnosing autism can be difficult.

Autism resembles other disorders of behaviour, communication and learning and so various other possible conditions need to be excluded before a diagnosis of autism can be made.

As it is relatively rare, most professionals aren't familiar enough with it to diagnose it easily. In the UK, the National Autistic Society (NAS) aims to combat this with five-day courses designed to educate health professionals about the condition.

Apart from anything else, doctors who are not specialists in developmental disorders are often reluctant to label a child as autistic if they are unsure because the diagnosis is so upsetting to parents and will have a lifelong impact on the child. They would rather not give a diagnosis than get it wrong.

Unfortunately, there are no medical tests for diagnosing autism, though this may happen one day (see the box later in this chapter, How young can a child be diagnosed?). Routine blood and/or urine tests, scans and other tests all tend to come back normal, especially in milder cases of autism.

Accurate diagnoses can only be made by questioning parents, observing how the child communicates and behaves and seeing what developmental stage he or she has reached. Your input is a very important part of making an accurate diagnosis. You may be asked lots of questions about your child's development and capabilities, language testing and evaluation.

Many of the characteristic traits of autism are also found in other disorders, such as language or hearing disorders, behaviour disorders or learning difficulties, so these also need to be excluded during the diagnostic process. To make it even more complicated, such conditions can coexist with autism.

All this means that not only may diagnosis take some time, but that various medical tests may be carried out to exclude other possible causes of your child's symptoms.

Can you tell if it's autism?

Many young children (say two to three years old) may display autistic traits at times. They may still be very egocentric and interested more in their own activities than in others. Their sociability may vary depending on their development. For example, a child learning to run or jump may be so fascinated by that that he does not want to interact with other children too much. Children of this age may not yet have learned to play with other children – at least not for sustained periods of time.

Some children just don't want to play imaginative games and naturally prefer slightly more 'mechanical' games involving numbers or letters.

Seeing your doctor

You may have to push for an early referral for assessment by a community paediatrician, child and adolescent mental health services, together with Social Services, speech and language therapists, and preschool special educational needs teachers. Dr Lorna Wing advises parents not to be fobbed off by family doctors who dismiss their worries with a verdict of glue ear or similar, but to insist on a swift referral to a paediatrician, psychiatrist or psychologist with a known interest in autism. Parents know their own child best.

If your doctor is unwilling to refer your child for specialist help, there are various actions that you can take.

- Keep a behavioural diary for your child and note down any symptoms that worry you. In particular, look for symptoms of autism (as detailed below).
- Prepare notes before your visit so you can argue your case better.
- Supply the practice or your GP with information on autism from an information and support group, such as the National Autistic Society (see the Useful addresses section at the back of the book).
- Ask to see another doctor if it is a group practice.
- Seek a second opinion, with the agreement of your GP.
- Ask to see a consultant of your choice, with the agreement of your GP.

Equally, many toddlers and even slightly older children are routine freaks and protest loudly when the usual way of doing things is changed. Having things a certain way or even in a certain order contributes to their sense of security. Finally, young children are notoriously active and difficult to control.

So how do you spot autism? High-functioning autism in particular may be missed. In older children, it may be mistaken for behaviour problems because affected children can become so frustrated and no one asks why.

The main areas to consider are speech and understanding. Does your child obey simple commands – for example, when you ask him to fetch a toy? Many children understand well long before they can talk. If he cannot understand (and is not choosing to ignore), then hearing might be a problem rather than autism.

Definite signs to heed include:

- no babbling by 12 months
- your child does not respond to her name
- appearing deaf some of the time
- no gesturing (pointing or waving) by the age of one
- no single words by 16 months
- not following simple commands – 'Bring me the teddy, please', for example – by 18 months
- no spontaneous two-word sentences (for communication, not simply repetition of what you are saying) by two years
- any loss of language at any age.

These warning signs do not necessarily mean that your child has autism, but they are indications that your child should be further evaluated.

Some parents, however, prefer not to go through the diagnostic procedure. Especially if their child is able, they may prefer not to have him labelled, and don't wish him to be pinned down by a diagnosis.

Edward had always been slightly odd. He had a quaint, pedantic way of talking in which he adapted quotes from books he had read, such as *Alice in Wonderland*. At six, he was a delicate-looking, pallid boy, sociable enough about the things that interested him (drains, biology and space travel), but otherwise rather remote.

His mother, feeling that he would not survive secondary school, withdrew him and his (much more robust) sister and decided to educate them at home. She was able to abandon the limits of the National Curriculum and direct Edward's often detailed interests into a much wider education.

There was never any question of taking Edward to the doctor for a diagnosis of his sometimes irritating peculiarities. His mother felt that she could accept Edward on his own terms and create a society in which he could mix more comfortably. Through Education Otherwise, the UK organization for parents educating their children at home, they kept in touch with a number of families in the same position as themselves. At 14, Edward is still being educated at home and is happy, although his mother admits that she cannot imagine what he will do when he is an adult.

While you're waiting
You don't have to wait for a definitive diagnosis of autism before you take action.
- Find help and support. Look for local and national support groups, such as the NAS, which has groups nationwide.
- Inform yourself about autism via books, groups and the Internet. Be selective with the latter, though.
- Access information from adults who are autistic, who can tell you how it feels from the inside. Professor Temple Grandin and Dr Wendy Lawson are both highly successful autistic people who have written extensively about the condition. (See the Further reading and Useful addresses sections at the back of the book.)
- Think about ways in which you can start to help your child. One way to improve communication skills is to build up a series of picture cards to help him express feelings and intentions.

When to think about having your child diagnosed

When should a child with autism be diagnosed? The earlier the better is the answer to this question, because research indicates that early diagnosis can mean a much better outcome for a child with autism.

Young children have more neurons than adults, which make it possible for them to acquire language and social skills. After around seven years of age, neuronal connections or pathways that are not used disappear, while the connections that are used (for example, for speech) are strengthened. This isn't to say a child can't learn after this age – it just takes longer. However, it makes sense to take advantage of this phase to start 'rewiring' the young brain.

So, the sooner autism is diagnosed, the sooner your child can begin benefiting from help and treatment specifically designed for autism. Intensive early intervention has been shown to improve speech, intellectual progress and general development in up to 75 per cent of children with autism.

Depending on whether or not your child has any other condition, it may also be important to ensure that he receives the right medical care, too.

Early diagnosis is important for more than just the child. It helps put support for the family in place and reduces family stress. One study showed that the way in which a diagnosis was presented to parents had a major impact on their acceptance of the situation, their long-term attitudes, stress and general coping.

Early diagnosis is also vital because then parents can have access to genetic counselling if they are planning to have other children. They may need to know for the sake of any brothers and sisters their child already has as the genetic component of autism makes for an increased risk of siblings being affected, so they may need extra help, too. Siblings might appear to be less affected than their brother or sister, but have real problems in areas such as social interaction or communication. Again, help could be given to them, too.

Similar conditions

Some conditions can be confusingly similar to autism so careful exploration of any problems is needed before a diagnosis of autism is made.

In general, any condition that may be associated with language delay merits further investigation. Also, some conditions can coexist with autism, such as mental retardation, though in this case the child often has more social and communication skills than one who has autism.

Other possible coexisting conditions include epilepsy, cerebral palsy, Down's syndrome or other chromosomal disorders, dyslexia, general learning difficulties and visual or hearing impairment.

Hearing loss is one of the first conditions that should be excluded before autism is diagnosed. Indeed, many parents of autistic children are at first concerned that their child is deaf. A hearing test will establish whether or not your child can hear normally. This is especially important to do with young children to rule out glue ear, which can persist for months. This causes temporary hearing problems, but may have an impact on development and behaviour. (However, don't be fobbed off by your doctor with a diagnosis of glue ear if you think there is more to it than that.)

Instant diagnosis

With more than 2000 children being diagnosed with autism a year in the UK, those working in local mental health services must be better trained to detect autism, says Professor David Skuse of the Institute of Child Health.

Professor Skuse's own computerized test, which asks parents 140 questions about their child's strengths and difficulties in a standardized, quickly analysed way, usually aids him in making a same-day diagnosis. He is also able to tell parents where their child is on the autistic spectrum (how autistic they are) and what the future may hold.

Professor Skuse's clinic at Great Ormond Street Children's Hospital is the only clinic in the UK to offer a pre-clinic home visit and follow-up assessment at school. A psychologist from the clinic sees children at home aged from 2 to 16 in 80 families across Britain. This cuts waiting times for new appointments from five months to just two weeks.

A course at the Institute of Child Health has been designed to train 150 health professionals a year, including paediatricians, psychiatrists and clinical psychologists, to spot high-functioning autistic children at a younger age and identify what help they need.

Ideally, the next step is to have consistently adequate, efficient continuing care available from all local education and health services across the UK, though, sadly, this is far from the case.

A child with a hearing problem will not necessarily have all the classic features of autism, but may tend to ignore people around him, make unusual speech sounds and have poor eye contact because he won't be looking in the direction of the sound. There may also be temper tantrums due to the frustration caused by not being able to express his needs. However, once any deafness has been treated, a child will quickly recover any lost language. Even if you, his parents, think he can hear, it is wise to have a test as the child may be attuned to the frequencies of your voices or the hearing loss may be partial.

Attention deficit hyperactivity disorder (ADHD), which involves hyperactivity and inattention, may sometimes be confused with or diagnosed with autism. However, children with ADHD tend to develop social and communication skills as they grow older and become calmer, while a child with autism will tend to become more withdrawn.

Landau Kleffner Syndrome (LKS), or acquired epileptiform aphasia, is a relatively rare condition that involves seizures and loss of speech. The seizure activity involves the left hemisphere of the brain, in which the speech areas are located. This means that the child suffers progressive loss of speech (aphasia), which may first appear as deafness, with the child's parents having increasing difficulty in getting a response from the child, even when they raise their voices. The child's speech may then deteriorate, losing words that she has already learned or using just one or two words or unrecognizable jargon. Behaviour problems sometimes develop.

Your family doctor can refer your child for an EEG to test for abnormal brain activity if this disorder is suspected. It can be treated with anticonvulsant drugs.

Rett syndrome is a comparatively rare, complicated neurological disorder that affects girls. A child may seem to develop normally until between 6 and 18 months of age, then regress. The cause is known to be a genetic disorder. This regression is followed by a deceleration of head growth, loss of purposeful hand movements, followed by the appearance of stereotypical hand movements.

Selective mutism is when a child will speak in some situations but not others (typically, a child will talk at home but not at school). Although some children with autism are mute, they will be mute in all, not just some, situations. Unlike in autism, selective mutism may also have a psychological component. For example, a child who is close to his mother and has never attended preschool may be traumatized by his first day at school and so not speak.

Other conditions with a psychiatric component include, very rarely, schizophrenia and obsessive-compulsive disorder.

Specific developmental disorders – particularly language-related ones – may sometimes mimic autism. However, children with such disorders have social skills and don't usually have the restricted interests of a child with autism.

How autism is diagnosed

A doctor experienced in autism may be able to make a diagnosis the second a child enters the room. For example, Dr Lorna Wing has described times when she has been able to do this, such as when a child comes rushing in and starts lining up all the fridge magnets. Equally, many doctors may know intuitively that something is wrong, but don't have the expertise in developmental disorders to say exactly what. So how is autism diagnosed?

The classic triad of impairments mentioned earlier is used as a basis for diagnosing autism – that is, problems with communication and social interactions, as well as repetitive behaviour and narrow interests.

In order to create a universal standard for the diagnosis of autism among other conditions, experts have created lists of criteria. The most widely used are the *Diagnostic and Statistical Manual of Mental Disorders*, 4th edition (DSM-IV), and the *International Classification of Diseases*, 10th edition (ICD-10). The criteria in these books are very similar.

Several screening tests focus on key areas of development and early academic skills, such as speech and language and fine and gross motor skills, or, in older children, general knowledge, reading and mathematics. Some, though not all, of these tests are as follows.

- **Childhood Autism Rating Scale (CARS)** This was developed by Eric Schopler in the early 1970s and is based on observed behaviour. A 15-point scale is used to evaluate your child's relationship to other people, body use, adaptation to change, listening response and verbal communication.
- **Checklist for Autism in Toddlers (CHAT)** This test is used to screen for autism at 18 months of age. It was developed by Simon Baron-Cohen in the early 1990s to see if autism could be detected in children as young as 18 months. The screening tool uses a short questionnaire with two sections – one prepared by the parents, the other by the child's family doctor or paediatrician. In particular, it focuses on areas such as pretend play, gaze monitoring and proto-

How young can a child be diagnosed?
Doctors are working on screening tools to help bring down the
age at which autism can be identified. One research study used
home videos to pick out specific ways of behaving in babies
with autism. Four key areas of behaviour were identified:

● eye contact
● responding to their name being called
● pointing
● showing.

Other work suggests that similar patterns of behaviour can be
identified at younger ages, too.

Most revolutionary of all, however, is a pilot study in
America that found that newborns at risk of autism could be
identified by blood samples. This finding raises exciting
possibilities for future screening and treatment for a condition
that, as we have seen so far, is classically diagnosed from
behaviour traits.

The researchers found that babies with autism or mental
retardation had strikingly higher levels of four specific proteins
that are crucial to nervous system development. The four
proteins are known to have a role in regulating the growth and
development of the brain during pregnancy and contribute to
long-term memory, learning and responses to sensory stimuli.
The study was conducted by the California Birth Defects
Monitoring Program (CBDMP) of the California Department
of Health Services and the National Institutes of Health (NIH).

declarative pointing (a prespeech gesture used by older babies and
toddlers to declare an interest in something).
● **Autism Screening Questionnaire** This is a 40-item screening
scale that has been used with children aged four and older to help
evaluate communication skills and social functioning.
● **Screening Test for Autism in Two-year-olds** This is being
developed by Wendy Stone at Vanderbilt University, Tennessee,
specifically to differentiate autism from other developmental

disorders. Dr Stone has identified three areas that seem to indicate autism – play (both pretend and reciprocal social play), motor imitation and non-verbal communication.

There is no harm in approaching your doctor if you are at all worried. These days, many parents are bringing up children without the help and support of their extended families, which means that they may have no one to tell them whether certain behaviour and development is normal or not. An important part of a health professional's job is to provide reassurance or, if there is still some doubt, refer you for any further investigations to find out more. Neither of these can come too early, for your peace of mind and for the future of your child.

5
Treatments

This is a minefield. If the world of the child with autism is confusing, so is the world of the parent trying to unravel the mass of treatments for it! Parents ask, 'Can't the doctor prescribe my child some drug? Should we try vitamins and, if so, which ones? What about secretin and where can I get hold of it?' Then there are the behavioural and educational programmes, which are legion – their adherents all hotly claiming that theirs is the only one that works.

To make matters worse, every treatment for autism has its critics and it is a known fact that no one treatment works for every single child. To add to the confusion, some children with autism appear to experience remission or improve spontaneously without any apparent treatment.

Where to start? Once the diagnosis has been made, parents have to cope with the fact that there is no definitive treatment for autism – no chemotherapy on which to get your child swiftly started, no operation to book him in for. Yet, all the research says that starting some form of treatment or therapy early on can be important in helping to maximize your child's language, social skills and behaviour. While this cannot cure autism itself, it can minimize the build-up of secondary behavioural problems.

Left to themselves, autistic children may make significantly less progress than is possible with treatment. The initial aim is to break through (gently) the child's social barriers and for them to establish communication with others, whether this be by means of pointing, using pictures or sign language, as well as speech.

Just as the children are all individuals, so treatment needs to be customized to each child's needs. Unfortunately, this often means a process of trial and error, parents learning to depend less on the doctor and more on themselves. You may well find that a combination of approaches works best, such as a mixture of behavioural therapy and diet. There may be times when you have to use medication as well.

While shopping around is not recommended, rigidly sticking to one treatment may not always be the best idea either. Your child may quickly gain all he is going to from one approach, after which it may be time to move on. The aim with an autistic child will always be to improve communication, tolerance of other people and quality of life.

It is worth being cautious when choosing treatment for your child. His personality is of prime importance in deciding on an approach – how much he can tolerate, whether he is likely to enjoy the treatment and so on. You understand your child best. Don't be talked into an approach against your better judgement, especially if it strikes you as harsh, abusive or simply unsuitable for your child. For example, 'holding therapy' has frequently been advocated as a treatment for autism. This is where the child is gently restrained, say during a tantrum, while the holder tries to 'get in touch' with the child, but this may be unbearable to a child who has sensory difficulties of a tactile nature. Temple Grandin is one of several autistic people who have spoken out against this form of treatment.

Autism is generally spoken of as being a lifelong condition that is treatable, not curable. Bear in mind that you may not be able to judge the treatment in terms of how successful it has been in 'curing' your child's autism. However, if it has improved his quality of life, this is a substantial benefit that cannot be taken away from him. Some parents believe that their child's autism has indeed been cured. For example, Karyn Seroussi, a founder of Autism Network for Dietary Intervention (ANDI), has detailed how she and her husband cured their son Miles of autism by removing first dairy and then gluten products from his diet, but other parents have tried this without success. Of this, more in the next chapter.

There are also people who appear to have recovered from autism – they learn how to operate in the community and have a successful career. Many have to go through much social pain and confusion in the process of finding a state where they can be happy as themselves. This brings into focus the most important thing in all this – your child. Unless he is pressured to be 'normal', he may be happy with himself and with life. For many parents, part of the treatment is coming to terms with their child as he is.

One problem you don't have is the onus of feeling that you are responsible for your child's condition. The Italian *Rizzoli Larousse Encyclopedia* was forced to amend its entry on autism because of outrage caused by the original definition, which stated that upbringing could cause autism and that an autistic child could be cured if he received appropriate treatment that was 'followed up by his relatives (who are often the cause of the syndrome, especially when they overstep the mark and insist on an over-perfectionist upbringing)'.

Autism support groups were enraged that the outdated notion of a cold, unloving parent, or 'refrigerator mother', was still alive and kicking. In many ways, Freud – whose work obscured that of his fellow Viennese, Asperger – set neurology back for many decades.

Parents beware

As public knowledge of autism increases, so a wealth of new therapies and treatments has sprung up – some would say these are snake oil. Treatments certainly range widely, from music therapy and melatonin, to homeopathy and dolphin therapy!

Many parents find that – depending on what they can afford and what is available (how many parents in the UK have access to dolphin therapy?) – certain therapies do make a difference to their child's quality of life. However, parents looking for a cure for their child are vulnerable beings. Do watch out for:

- 'miracle' cures or claims from therapists that their way is your child's only hope
- anyone who believes that your child's autism is a result of poor parenting or an emotional disturbance
- professionals such as teachers, therapists and social workers working from outdated information – for example, anyone who believes that autism is an emotional disorder or who favours psychotherapy and psychoanalysis as therapies.

The National Institute of Mental Health's (NIMH) autism unit in the USA suggests asking the following questions before investing in any kind of treatment.

- How successful has the programme been for other children?
- How many children have gone on to placements in mainstream schools and how have they performed?
- Do staff members have training and experience in working with children and adolescents with autism?
- How are activities planned and organized?

- Are there predictable daily schedules and routines?
- How much individual attention will my child receive?
- How is progress measured? Will my child's behaviour be closely observed and recorded?
- Will my child be given tasks and rewards that are personally motivating?
- Is the environment designed to minimize distractions?
- Will the programme prepare me to continue the therapy at home?
- What are the costs, time commitment and location of the programme?

Which treatment?

Behavioural therapies are usually suggested as being the most successful type of treatment for ensuring that a child with autism gets the best possible start in life. They can help minimize exhausting and antisocial behaviour and make the most of your child's potential, which may be greater than anyone expects.

The best-known therapies – because of the amount of related scientific literature – are the Lovaas approach and TEACCH programme. Both are highly structured methods with a lot of positive reinforcement – two factors that seem to be important. Then there are neurosensory treatment programmes, designed to help those with sensory difficulties. These include sensorial integration, auditory training and facilitated communication, which are described below in more detail.

Drug treatment does exist and may help some children, especially if they have other conditions such as epilepsy, but parents often want to try other approaches first.

Biochemical treatments, such as testing for and treating food allergies, secretin, food and vitamin supplements, are covered in the next chapter.

Behavioural therapy

Behavioural therapy tries to reinforce 'good' behaviour and eliminate the 'bad'. The idea of modifying behaviour by means of therapy was originally developed by Dr B. F. Skinner, but was only later modified by several psychologists as a therapy for children with autism.

Modifying behaviour may be very useful – indeed essential – for some children with autism who might otherwise run wild and persevere in behaviour that might eventually have to be controlled by drugs or even lead to them having to live in an institution.

Behavioural therapies abound, but some of the more established methods are described below.

The TEACCH programme

It was started in north Carolina, USA, as a research project in the mid 1960s by Dr Eric Schopler. Now, TEACCH has developed into an internationally recognized method of treating those with autism.

TEACCH stands for Treatment and Education of Autistic and Related Communication Handicapped Children/Adults. The programme is based on the premise that many people with autism find it easier to process visual rather than spoken or written information.

The method can help not just with education but also life choices. For example, rather than asking a child whether he wants to go swimming or walking, a picture of each activity may be presented to him and he can point to one. As well as having the satisfaction of making a choice, it may also be clearer to the child what is going to happen next – important to those with autism, and especially when dealing with behavioural problems.

Structured teaching has had a wide impact as it helps to organize the children's environment, providing clear, concrete and meaningful visual information. Several studies have found that this has resulted in improved attending, relatedness, emotional warmth and general behaviour.

The Lovaas approach

Formulated by Dr Ivar Lovaas at UCLA, USA, this approach teaches children new skills in small steps. The aim is that they should succeed 90 per cent of the time and the focus is on getting into their minds and finding ways to make contact so that new material is given to them in a way that they will find easy and fun.

Research indicates that this therapy improves communicative, cognitive and social abilities in 40–50 per cent of autistic children. However, critics claim that the method is somewhat severe and those participating in Lovaas' original studies in the late 1980s were not truly autistic.

SPELL

SPELL aims to provide a structured environment, a positive attitude with realistic expectations, empathy, seeing the world from the autistic person's viewpoint and low arousal, an environment and lifestyle that reduces stress and anxiety.

- S is for structure. The environment needs to be structured to help children make sense of their often confusing world. Structure also makes the real world safer for them as it helps to prevent or reduce the incidence of unexpected events.
- P is for positive attitudes, which help to boost children's self-confidence. Expectations need to be high enough to inspire them without causing anxiety, but not so low as to cause boredom. Rewards and acknowledgement of success are also vital.
- E is for empathy. Trying to see the world from the children's point of view helps teachers to plan an education geared to their particular needs and anxieties.
- L is for low arousal. Many autistic children, because of their sensory differences, do not like noise or overly bright lights. A calm, organized environment helps to minimize distractions so that the children can focus better.
- L is also for links with parents, other agencies and schools. Hopefully, one day they can be included in a mainstream school.

PECS

This stands for 'picture exchange communication system'. It works on the basis that people with autism tend to be visual learners who think in pictures rather than words. It uses objects, picture symbols, photos and written words to help children communicate. It was developed by Dr Andrew Bondy and Lori Frost at the Delaware Autistic Program in the USA.

The NAS's EarlyBird Programme

This is a three-month programme of workshops, home visits and video feedback training, designed to teach parents how to best support their young children. The course aims to help parents understand their child's autism, aid communication and prevent and handle behaviour problems. It draws on approaches from SPELL, TEACCH and PECS, described above.

Neurosensory treatments

Neurosensory therapies try to treat problems arising from abnormal sensory reactions, which are experienced by so many with autism. They vary very widely, so it is beyond the scope of this book to cover them all. However, some of the main ones can be summarized as follows.

Auditory integration training (AIT)
This involves listening to specially adapted music via headphones, the aim of which is to change the listener's sensitivity to sounds of different frequencies. Originally developed as a treatment for deafness, it has been shown to reduce symptoms of autism in some children.

The theory is that autistic people are overly sensitive to certain sounds, yet do not pick up others very well. In particular, some autistic children cannot bear certain sounds and AIT has helped them to increase their toleration of these.

The imbalance in their hearing is analysed and the music adapted to retrain the ear. This, in turn, improves speech and behaviour.

There are various methods for implementing AIT. The Tomatis method involves listening to classical music with the low frequencies filtered out. Over time, voices (also filtered out at first) are introduced, then the missing frequencies.

Facilitated communication (FC)
In FC, a facilitator lightly supports the hand or arm to help the autistic child press a keyboard to spell out her thoughts. The keyboard may consist of letters or be a communication picture board.

FC is viewed as an alternative means of expression for people who either cannot speak or whose speech is limited. Care has to be taken that it is the autistic person making the choice of letter or picture, not the facilitator. Indeed, there has been some controversy about this form of treatment precisely because of this difficulty. However, supporters say that FC does indeed communicate the thoughts of a person otherwise unable to speak, helps increase communication, builds trust with the child and so improves behaviour.

47

Sensory integration therapy
This is a method of helping those who are over- or undersensitive by providing them with carefully controlled sensory experiences. The aim, naturally, is to get the child to tolerate troublesome experiences better.

Sensory integration therapy aims to improve the way in which a child's brain responds to, and makes use of, sensory information and how this is used to plan, coordinate and organize movement. It also has a positive effect on self-confidence and self-esteem.

Other neurosensory treatments
These include 'daily life therapy', pioneered in Japan and adapted in some treatment centres in Europe, and Doman/Delacato (developed by Glenn Doman and Carl Delacato), which involve brain stimulation activities for brain-injured children (see the Useful addresses section at the back of the book for website address).

Drug treatment

There is no one drug that is used to treat autism. Indeed, many professionals feel that it does not achieve much to put a child on medication. Professor Michael Rutter of the Maudsley Hospital, London, has come to the conclusion – repeating earlier findings – that there is no drug that produces major behavioural improvements in cases of autism.

However, depending on a child's difficulties, some drugs may help with aspects of his problems. For example, a third of children with autism also suffer from seizures, in which case anticonvulsant medication may be useful. Modern antidepressants, such as the SSRIs, have made a difference for some children, relieving the often overwhelming anxiety some can suffer. Ritalin has also been widely tried, especially in the USA, with children who are deemed to be hyperactive, but this is a controversial and, some say, ineffective drug.

If you are considering drug treatment, try to discuss it fully with a doctor experienced in autism before proceeding. There is some evidence that children with autism process drugs differently from those whose neuronal development has been normal. It is difficult enough to foretell what the effects of drugs will be on a person with a 'normal' central nervous system, but, bearing in mind that autism is an organic condition, drugs may have even more of an unknown impact on the brain of an autistic child. Your doctor may have to go through a process of trial and error before finding the medication, or combination of them, that works best for your child.

6

Biochemical and other therapies

There has been a tremendous amount written about the benefits of the right diet for children with autism. As well as certain exclusion diets – diets that cut out a particular food, such as wheat or dairy products – supplementation with vitamins and secretin, a digestive hormone, have been tried with some success.

The dietary treatments are based on a specific view of autism (as explained further on in this chapter) and some parents swear by them, believing that they have indeed cured their child's autism. Sadly, others have tried them with no effect. Perhaps it is the case that certain diets may help some children, especially if they have intolerances to certain ingredients as well as autism or if they are deficient in some vitamins. Whether they can actually cure autism or not is less sure, although many parents report that they have dramatically improved their child's behaviour and sociability. The exclusion diets do involve dedication, but many parents feel that the results are well worth all the trouble.

As with all aspects of the management of your child's condition, care should be taken before investing in an expensive, little-validated treatment or therapy. Also, if you do decide, after seeking sound advice, to go ahead, try one approach at a time so you can assess how well it works.

Elimination diets

Some parents have found that eliminating certain foods from their child's diet brings about a huge improvement and lessens picky eating. Foods commonly blamed are sugar, food additives, colourings and caffeine. In particular, a diet free of gluten or dairy products has been reported as having dramatic beneficial effects on some children.

Keep a food diary to see if your child's behaviour changes after eating certain foods. For example, he may become more active or frenetic or display allergy-related symptoms, such as a runny nose, hayfever or dark circles beneath his eyes. Try eliminating suspected culprit foods for at least two weeks to see if it makes a difference.

If you can get your child to tolerate it, dietary management is certainly something that you can try at home, though it is a good idea to get a sympathetic doctor or nutritionist to supervise the process if you possibly can to ensure that your child still has a balanced diet with all the necessary nutrients. Exclusion diets are troublesome and time-consuming, and you will probably appreciate as much back-up as possible. You can also obtain this via the Internet (visit the ANDI website – its address is given in the Useful addresses section at the back of the book).

The idea that the right diet could improve autistic symptoms began in 1980 when scientist Jaak Panksepp observed that autistic children had many traits in common with people addicted to opiates. Like some children with autism, addicts are often 'in their own world' and may exhibit particular behaviour, such as rocking, insensitivity to pain and gastrointestinal problems. Panksepp proposed that autistic children might have elevated levels of naturally occurring opiates in their central nervous systems.

More recently, Paul Shattock, Head of the University of Sunderland's Autism Research Unit, has created a urine test to measure the levels of opiate-like peptides that autistic children excrete and has found that 50 per cent of people with autism seem to have high levels of these substances.

The theory is that gluten (in wheat) and dairy products 'drug' autistic children in the same way as morphine. Tiny proteins from these food substances (peptides) leak into the gut and act like opiates, dampening brain activity in some children. Both gluten (found in wheat, rye, barley and most oat products) and casein (in dairy products) produce these proteins in the body.

Casein produces the peptide casomorphine, which acts like an opiate, while gluten compounds form gluteomorphins, adding to the level of opiate-like substances in the body. Parents' reports and research seem to indicate that some children cannot break down these proteins properly.

Tom practically lived on milk and wheat – his diet revolved around milk, cheese, cereal, pasta and bread. The nutritionist who saw Tom told his mother Beth that Tom was addicted to the foods containing the proteins casein and gluten, as opiates are highly addictive.

Tom was started on an elimination diet, beginning with pears, rice and meat – typically viewed as foods that are the least likely to cause adverse reactions. After an initial withdrawal reaction, Tom began to eat other foods. 'We went through a touchy three weeks with loads of tantrums and then suddenly came out the other side,' says Beth. 'Tom behaves so much better now. And it is infinitely preferable to him being dosed up with drugs with all their horrible side-effects.'

Removing dairy products means no milk, butter, cheese, cream cheese, sour cream, as well as products with ingredients such as 'casein' and 'whey' on the labels, and even words containing the word 'casein', such as 'caseinate'. Read labels carefully as items such as bread and tuna fish often contain milk products.

The practicalities

Parents are often daunted by the task of removing all gluten and dairy from their child's diet. Walk down the aisles in any supermarket and you will see that most of the food seems to consist mainly of flour and dairy products. To make matters worse, gluten is a product that is often hidden in foods such as soups, sauces, cereals and pre-prepared foods.

Advocates of the diet stress that total elimination of these products is the best way to achieve success. So where do you start?

- Try to eliminate dairy products first before moving on to gluten. Casein is found in all forms of dairy products, such as cheese, creams, butter, yogurt, ice cream and sauces. You will need to read labels to check for all dairy ingredients, including the less obvious ones such as whey, caseinate and so on.
- To make life easier, look for gluten-free and casein-free foods in your supermarket or order them online.
- Aim to try the diet for at least one month – three if you can manage it.
- Expect your child to get worse before he gets better as his system protests at the removal of the foods he is used to.
- Get support from your doctor, health visitor, nutritionist or autism support group.

The serotonin factor

There is speculation that some children with autism may have too much serotonin in their brains – a condition known as hyperserotonemia.

Which children respond to elimination diets best?
Two doctors in the UK who advocate exclusion diets are Consultant Paediatrician Michael Tettenborn, of Fimley Children's Hospital, and John Richer, of the John Radcliffe Hospital, Oxford. Both have had success with autistic children on these diets.

Unfortunately, exclusion diets do not work for all children with autism. They seem to have more of an effect on children who show signs of food intolerances, such as pallor or redness of the skin, dark shadows under the eyes, catarrh, a runny nose, nose bleeds or even snoring. Other symptoms may be cravings for specific foods (for example, pasta or cheese), bloating, diarrhoea, often being thirsty, eczema, asthma, hayfever or other allergies.

Children who seem to respond best to a dairy-free diet may have a history of ear infections, inconsolable crying, poor sleeping patterns and excessive craving of milk and dairy foods.

A gluten-free diet may be most helpful for children who suffer from irritable bowel syndrome and those who have cravings for bread and pasta. However, you will need to experiment to see which diet, if any, suits your child best.

One really important point: even if the diets do result in an improvement and even though your child may become physically better as his brain clears, he may well need further help to 're-learn' life skills such as playing, learning or even – most basic of all – bonding with you. So, don't leave the diets to do all the work – have some back-up plans available to work on the whole child, not just his physical wellbeing.

Review the research treatments outlined in the previous chapter, too, talk to your doctor and other parents, join an autism support group and generally be prepared to help your child re-enter life if the diet has a positive effect.

Serotonin is a neurotransmitter that acts on the brain to influence motivation and mood, and some foods are more likely than others to help in its manufacture. These tend to be foods that are high in carbohydrates, such as pasta, starchy vegetables, potatoes, cereals and bread.

Carbohydrates enhance the absorption of tryptophan, which is converted into serotonin in the brain. It is inadvisable to experiment in this area without your doctor or nutritionist's advice, but you could try cutting down on or eliminating sugar in all forms, including in drinks, cakes and sweets. Instead, give your child complex carbohydrates, such as wholemeal bread and brown rice, instead of simple ones, such as white bread, rice and pasta. Ensure, too, that he eats some protein at every meal – eggs, cheese, meat, fish or legumes (beans, lentils, chickpeas and so on), for example.

General diet tips

It's important that your child doesn't become a tyrant when it comes to food and meals and spoils family times together. Try these general tips for regular, healthy eating – for the whole family, not just your autistic child!

- When shopping, don't buy sweets, cakes, biscuits and junk foods – if they're not in the house, no one can eat them.
- Give your child three meals a day with healthy morning and afternoon snacks, such as fresh or dried fruit, crackers or popcorn. He may also need a bedtime snack.
- Try to ensure that he sits down at the table with the family rather than in front of the TV or wandering around the house. Reward him for sitting down at first if this works better.
- Even if he has rigid food fads, offer a variety of healthy foods.
- Give him the freedom to choose what and how much to eat. Try placing food in several serving dishes with serving spoons, rather than simply putting a plate of food in front of him.
- Give plain water or milk as drinks (substituting soya milk if you suspect that he reacts to casein).
- Save sweet desserts for an occasional treat and put out fruit instead.
- Increase picky eaters' interest in meals by involving him in the preparation of the meal.
- If your child continues to be a very fussy eater, consult your doctor, who may recommend supplements.

Vitamin therapy

Vitamin therapy has been used for autism since the 1960s. It has been strongly advocated by the American psychologist Dr Bernard Rimland, Director of the Autism Research Institute, San Diego, California, and founder of the American Society of Autism. Results have been varied, according to several studies, but these supplements are more likely to help if your child is deficient in the particular vitamin.

The main vitamins that have been tried are vitamins A, B6 and C. Vitamin A may help people with autism, especially those with vision, sensory perception, language processing and attention problems. Don't overdo it, though, as too much vitamin A can lead to toxicity, causing liver problems and reduced bone mineral density that may result in osteoporosis. In pregnant women, excess intake of vitamin A may cause birth defects. So, either eat moderate amounts of foods containing vitamin A – the best way to take it – or, if taking supplements, do not exceed the recommended daily dose of 800 micrograms (2664 iu). Vitamin A can be found in cold water fish, such as salmon and cod, as well as liver, kidney, milk fat and cod liver oil. While this is unlikely to apply to your child, just in case you decide to take it, too, it is important to know that supplements shouldn't be taken if pregnant or planning pregnancy.

Vitamin B6 is often given with magnesium to reduce the risk of side-effects, such as numbness and tingling in the hands and feet. It has been suggested that it reduces hyperactivity and obsessive/compulsive behaviour. Vitamin B6 (pyridoxine) has been proved beneficial in around 50 per cent of those who try it. If you want to improve your child's intake without actually giving supplements, good food sources of vitamin B6 include potatoes, breakfast cereals, bread, meat, fish, eggs, baked beans, bananas, nuts and seeds, especially sunflower seeds.

Vitamin C helps the brain to function properly. Symptoms of deficiency include depression and confusion, both of which afflict autistic people. Good sources of vitamin C include citrus fruits, such as oranges, lemons, limes and grapefruits, vegetables, including red and green peppers, broccoli, Brussels sprouts, tomatoes, asparagus, parsley, dark leafy greens and cabbage, and other fruits, such as kiwi fruit, guavas, rosehips and blackcurrants.

Secretin

Secretin has caused a furore in the world of autism but has yet to be scientifically approved.

A hormone that is naturally present in the pancreas, secretin's supposed effect on autism was first publicized by an American mother, Victoria Beck, of New Hampshire, when her five-year-old autistic son was given a drug for a stomach complaint. Lack of secretin contributes to digestive problems, so taking it is a common treatment for stomach complaints. This was followed by other cases where children with autism received secretin and it initially seemed to improve their social and language skills.

Why should a digestive juice impact a neurological disorder? The theory behind secretin is similar to that outlined above regarding exclusion diets. The thinking is that autism is the consequence of a metabolic disorder, in that the intestines do not break down and digest food properly. The partially digested food products can pass into the bloodstream and the brain, having a numbing effect.

Early trials led to hopes that secretin might prove a successful treatment, but later studies have not backed this up. At present neither the Medicines Control Agency in the UK nor the Federal Drugs Agency in the USA have approved secretin for use as a treatment for autism.

However, this has not stopped the secretin story from rolling on. Research continues into the possible link between secretin and improved communication and social skills in autism. Many parents are still prepared to pay for its use as a treatment for their child.

One remedy tried by some is a homeopathic form of secretin, though again this has not been clinically tested and is not guaranteed to work. In the UK, this is available from Ainsworth's Homoeopathic Pharmacy in London (see the Useful addresses section at the back of the book for contact details).

7

Social communication – helping your child

Autistic conditions are sometimes described as disorders of empathy, or empathic disorders in the USA – a term that highlights the underdeveloped social skills associated with the condition. Contrary to common perceptions, this is an area where improvement is possible. Many autistic people learn social understanding and warmth or to communicate in effective ways even if they initially lack the foundations for social skills, such as the ability to read the non-verbal cues. This may happen in many ways – not just via speech.

This chapter looks at a variety of ways in which your child may be helped, from strategies that you may be able to use at home to improve communication to therapies that may help your child communicate non-verbally and feel generally more comfortable in the world.

What holds back social communication?

Children with autism, as noted above, are said to lack empathy, or understanding of how others may be feeling – what psychologists call a theory of mind. Many children with autism appear not to realize how their words and behaviour can impact others. The same is true of many 'normal' adults and children, of course! However, an autistic child may differ from the usual pattern in that she may not be able to learn how others feel, though with support and patience, some children do improve their understanding.

A child with autism may lack a wider concept of social behaviour, including the ability to process the non-verbal aspects of social communication, such as how to use eye contact, body posture and gesture.

Another problem can be the child's belief that her parents can read her mind, which puts the onus on the parent to be constantly alert to their child's needs. However, at some point your child needs to know how to communicate her needs to a wider world, not just you.

Bear in mind that communicating may be more important than

speaking. Some children learn to speak very late, others not at all; still others vary in how much they can actually say at different times.

Even if their speech does develop, there may still be problems both with the mechanics of speech and deeper communication issues. For example, some children speak in a 'dead' or neutral or singsong tone of voice, putting emphasis on the wrong syllables. Some children have problems expressing simple needs and desires – a difficulty exemplified by the story of the autistic young man who drank from the toilet bowl rather than ask for a glass of water. For these reasons, developing communication may be much more important than developing speech.

The foundations of good communication

- **Routine** Children with autism tend to need predictability (see also Chapter 8, Everyday living). A familiar routine helps reduce anxiety and attendant behaviour problems so that children are freer to concentrate on other aspects of life, such as communicating, learning and enjoying themselves.
- **Play** Play is the classic way to communicate socially with your child. Like other children, children with autism learn primarily through play and this learning includes vocabulary. While play may be limited or difficult for your child, you may find it possible to play on her terms. This means entering her world and joining her at play. You may then be able to expand on it and introduce some variety, so that she goes beyond the confines of any repetitive behaviour and ritual. For example, you can roll a ball with your child and then try throwing it or rolling it into another room.
- **Simple rewards** Ideally these should not be sweets, though many parents find that they do work! What you use very much depends on your child – she may not appreciate verbal praise, but you could give her more time to do a favourite activity, for example.

Talking with your child

Trying to communicate with your autistic child can often be a frustrating guessing game. Is she hungry, hot, thirsty? How can you get her to take in what you say, whether it's preparing for an outing or absorbing safety information about a hot cooker?

Wanting a child to speak is a very understandable aim. Likewise, using words to her is natural, but words may only get you so far and need to be backed up by other forms of communication, such as gestures, as described below under the heading 'Extra communication'. The need to give your child simple, clear instructions has already been mentioned. Studies have found that autistic people have problems with registering, processing and responding to external stimuli. Because of this, information and instructions (or even conversational remarks) need to be given simply, repetitively and in small bursts, using only the necessary words.

- Always use the same words for objects and activities.
- Use the same instructions each time when teaching new skills.
- Verbal praise for good work or behaviour may not mean much to some children with autism. You may need to find other ways in which to reward your child, such as extra time to play with a favourite toy.
- Try to keep communication simple and to the point, using only necessary words.
- Leave time after speaking so that your child has a chance to think and take in what you have just said.
- Maintain eye contact when you can, but never force it.
- Avoid sarcasm and figures of speech such as 'I nearly died laughing' as autistic children tend to take such phrases literally.
- At some point, though, you may need to explain these figures of speech, such as 'spend a penny'.
- Don't give in to inappropriate forms of communication, such as punching or pulling you around.

Listening to your child
There are different ways in which to listen to your child, because he may communicate in different ways. Some more able children can talk well about their needs. Others may communicate more by their behaviour. It may help to look at behaviour that you find irritating or unacceptable, such as rituals or violence, and ask if there is a message behind it. Violent, angry behaviour may be a sign that some needs are going unmet.

Extra communication

As some children with autism learn better when information is presented visually as well as verbally, use as many means of communication as possible – gestures, pictures, symbols, sign language, technology. Build communication into daily routines by combining the spoken word with photographs, symbols or gestures to help your child make his needs and feelings known.

Social stories

These are a way in which to teach children unwritten social rules, body language and facial expressions – all the signals that people use in social interactions, but which a child with autism may not recognize. They work by focusing on and explaining the subtle cues in social situations and suggesting appropriate responses.

Social stories use photographs, pictures and words to illustrate these social rules in different situations. For example, they could deal with fire safety and related topics such as smoke detectors, fire drills, fire alarms and touching fire or they might deal with a social situation, such as meeting a new person, going to a party, asking the way, waiting in line at a shop or taking turns in the playground. (See the Useful addresses section at the back of the book for sources of stories.)

Therapies that may help

Music therapy, vision therapy and support dogs may all be of benefit in fostering social communication, though they may not cure autism.

Music therapy

Music therapy has been accepted as helpful for autism since it was introduced to the UK in the 1950s and 1960s. Used to stimulate overall communication in those with autism, music is increasingly used as part of early treatment programmes for children with autism as it stimulates self-awareness, along with communication patterns that are similar to the early preverbal exchanges between parents and their babies, so vital to the development of social skills.

Making music involves many of the aspects of social interaction, such as self-awareness, self as related to others, shared play, taking turns, listening and responding to others. It allows children with autism to experience a wider range of changing emotions than usual, but within a secure structure. Some experts have speculated that music therapy may be a way in which children with autism can experience outside stimuli but without the pain of direct human contact. Some children with sensory problems may also benefit by increasing their tolerance of sound.

Vision therapy

Autistic behaviour is believed by some optometrists to relate to visual and perceptual problems, such as poor eye contact, difficulty attending visually, visual fixation and oversensitivity to light or colour.

This therapy is based on a definition of vision as not just sight, but the brain's ability to organize and interpret the information seen so that it becomes understandable or meaningful. Sensory input that is disorganized may result in disorganized and antisocial behaviour. Vision therapy aims to tackle poor social communication at its root.

How do you know if your child is likely to benefit? There are various clues, according to educational consultant Sally Brockett of the Avon Therapeutic Center for children, an autism centre in Connecticut in the USA.

Symptoms may include eyes that cross or turn, even a little, tilting the head or covering or closing an eye to look at objects or looking at things out of the corner or side of the eyes. Your child may also show signs of visual discomfort, such as blinking, grimacing or squinting, as well as visual stimulation activities, such as flicking her fingers, obsession with spinning, patterns or other visual effects or an interest in linear objects, such as counter edges or telephone wires.

Vision therapy is given by developmental or behavioural optometrists and involves retraining the visual system so that it functions better. This may involve follow-up exercises at home as well as sessions with the optometrist.

Treatment should also involve the use of developmental lenses during the session, which may include prisms to help achieve better visual alignment and processing or red or green filters. The optometrist should see the child and evaluate the lenses regularly. Glasses may also be used, with a positive reinforcement programme to help the child adjust if she has difficulty wearing them.

Service or support dogs

Some reports suggest that children with autism may be able to form bonds with animals more easily than with other humans. A few centres exist (mainly in the USA and Canada) that train dogs specifically for children with autism, enabling both them and their families to lead more independent lives. However, with patience, it may be possible for families themselves to train a puppy to help an autistic child.

Studies at Washington State University by Dr François Martin report that children with autism in 'dog-therapy sessions' experienced an increased interest in their environment and more interactions with the therapists and animals.

Autism assistance dogs, as they are sometimes called, may simply provide emotional and therapeutic support. Other reports, from families who have used trained service dogs (often Labradors), suggest that the children improve in many ways, showing increased eye contact and less stress-related behaviour generally and with the family. The families also report an often new ability to enjoy public outings. The dogs can also be trained to track down the child, should she leave home, and guide her safely back, avoiding such hazards as crossing busy streets.

It is much easier, as well as cheaper, to train a dog yourself at home, though it does involve a long-term commitment from parents while the dog is being trained – up to a year or more. It is usually recommended that the number of trainers be kept to a minimum – one if possible – to avoid confusing the animal.

When choosing a dog, you will obviously need to consider various factors, such as the animal's grooming, diet and veterinary needs. The dog's need for exercise and freedom should also be borne in mind so that the needs of the child and the dog are properly balanced. However, at the very least, you may gain a warm, supportive family pet – and walking it can only be good for the health of your autistic child and the rest of the family!

8
Everyday living

Living with autism is a daily challenge that calls for parents to use all their reserves of ingenuity, resourcefulness and sense of humour. Families find that they develop their own individual styles of coping, though this may be at the expense of the life that they had hoped to live. Traumas over activities and bedtime, though certainly not confined to families with an autistic child, can wreak havoc with the best-laid plans. Evolving a fairly dependable daily routine may help both you and your child.

Having a daily routine

One of the best-known facts about autism is the child's demand for routine and 'sameness'. Although it can be frustrating, a structured, familiar daily routine, with clear beginnings and endings, is important as your child will feel safe and in control and will perform best under familiar conditions.

It is important that the routine fits in as far as possible with your own needs and those of your family – again, this is an area where the child cannot be allowed to dominate the entire family. For now, you may need to warn your child clearly when you are about to change an activity – for example, 'Soon we are going out shopping.' Later, as she develops, you may be able to introduce some flexibility into a rigid routine, depending on how well your child tolerates it.

A regular routine may also be important in terms of good behaviour (see also Chapter 9, Behaviour and discipline). Rituals and obsessions can be very reassuring for your child, who may use them to cope with anxiety, stress and sensory experiences. On a good day you may be able to distract her, but on disrupted days you may just have to let it go.

You do not have to give up on expecting regular good behaviour from your child. However, it is important to see matters from her point of view and appreciate that what may not seem important to you can be vital to your child. Broken routines and unexpected changes mean that you may just have to live through 'one of those days'.

Your child will of course have to cope with major changes, such as a death in the family or moving house. However, she may not show distress or grief in the expected ways, such as crying or talking about it. Instead, you may notice changes of behaviour like those you might see in a preverbal toddler – a worsening of behaviour, sleep disruption, eating problems or an increase in aggression or anxiety. Don't underestimate the effect of permanent change on your child. She may need time and support to accustom herself to a rearranged life.

Bedtime and sleeping

Sleep disorders are a fact of life for many families with an autistic child. Either the child has trouble settling or wakes during the night or both.

Jack made a terrific fuss about going to bed. His parents traced his distress to the sound of the TV, which his father would watch while his mother struggled to put Jack to bed. They evolved a plan that consisted of keeping the house quiet – no TV, radio or washing machine on – while they both sat with Jack until he went to sleep. Eventually they progressed to having just one parent sitting with him, the other being able to leave the room.

Bella would wake screaming several times a night and her parents were becoming increasingly exhausted and desperate. Her mother tried several remedies and finally found that a night light (a luminous plug) and two heavy blankets instead of a duvet reduced Bella's waking, though it did not eliminate it entirely.

Sleep is an area where you can turn routine to your advantage in that strict timetabling up to bedtime may make it easier for your child to go to bed. Have specific times – in a set order – for the evening meal, wind-down time, bath. Keep it simple. If you don't have a clear routine at the moment, it may take your child several weeks to get used to it, but it is worth persevering.

Try keeping a sleep diary for two weeks in which you record not only how many hours of sleep your child is getting, but also other possible influences on sleep. These include diet, including stimulants such as sugar and food additives, exercise, any activities that seem to upset your child and so on.

Carol found that giving Sal a drink of orange squash in the

afternoon had a drastic effect on her – Sal would tear round the living room almost as if the furniture wasn't there, giggle a lot and generally be silly. The same happened with certain types of highly coloured sweets given after lunch (for more on diet, see Chapter 6).

Exercise (see also below for more on this subject) is certainly a useful way to ensure that your child is tired enough to sleep, but shouldn't be done too close to bedtime in case it overstimulates him (indeed, this applies to all of us). Mid-afternoon may be a good time, perhaps just after school if it can be managed.

Helping your child to wind down before bedtime is important – again, this applies to all children and adults! Some accounts by people with autism indicate that bedtime, sleep and the night can be concepts that cause anxiety or fear, so it is even more important to provide your child with a quiet time before bed. It can give you a chance to relax, too. Early evening is a classically stressful time because everyone is tired, there are probably meals to prepare and various family members to soothe and listen to, so it can take discipline not to rush around. Try to consciously use this time for everyone to relax, organize meals earlier in the day if you can, keep the radio and TV turned off and don't allow any noisy activities, if at all possible.

Exercise

Exercise is a generally underused therapy for children with autism who, sadly, often become overweight through lack of it. Several research studies have shown that vigorous exercise in particular can often improve challenging behaviour, such as stereotypical behaviour, hyperactivity, aggression and destructiveness. Mild exercise tends to have less of an effect.

Exercise has several other documented benefits on children with autism. Activities that use gross motor skills have been shown to improve clumsiness and stumbling. Exercise can also reduce stress and anxiety as well as improve sleep, reaction times and memory. Last, but by no means least, it can also help boost self-confidence – a lack of which is all too common in autistic children.

Making exercise part of your child's life may take a while and a huge effort – for some, it may be just too much trouble. However, if you can get help and support to take you through the transition to a

Relaxation techniques

Reports vary as to how effective relaxation techniques are. Some experts believe that they may cause autistic children more distress than anything – for example, an acutely touch-sensitive child may find a massage unbearable. There are ways round this if you care to try them, though you may have to persevere before your child accepts them. For example, stroking very lightly for short periods of time, massaging through clothes, massaging only the feet or head or using an oil with a smell the child likes (lavender is the traditional relaxant oil, but your child might like others).

Some reports indicate that cranio-sacral therapy can be soothing for children with autism and help them to sleep better. This treatment relies on the gentle manipulation of the bones to which the membranes surrounding the brain attach. One researcher found that it helped with three specific types of 'autistic' behaviour – head banging, hand chewing and vigorous thumb sucking. The full treatment is best administered by a qualified practitioner, but you could try gently massaging the back of your child's neck and head.

Some parents have found relaxation aids useful, such as music and natural sound cassettes. Others have found that their child creates her own relaxation technique, such as always listening to the same cassette. Having a lava lamp in the bedroom can be very helpful, too.

Like Jack and Bella described above, some children are exceptionally sensitive to sound, tactile things and light, so you might need to introduce changes such as thicker curtains and carpets or even move your child's bedroom to a quieter part of the house, if these adjustments will be tolerated. Heavier bedclothes may be reassuring to some (on the same principle as Temple Grandin's 'squeeze machine', which delivers a controllable amount of sensory pressure – see Chapter 8), but others may only be able to tolerate the lightest of bedclothes. As with all things, you know your child best, so try the ideas that will suit your child's likes and dislikes.

more active lifestyle, it can make an enormous difference to the quality of your child's life. Family and friends can help (have a written plan so everyone can be consistent in their approach) or consider professional tuition, so long as the teacher knows about autism.

You may find it helpful to have a few simple ways in which to use exercise to relieve your child's frustration. For example, show her how to run around the garden or park when she's angry or hit a ball across a tennis court or just how to jump up and down, scream into a pillow or hit a punch bag.

Organize your child's environment

Arranging the house so that it makes more sense to your child can be helpful. Furniture can be arranged to make everyday activities easier. For example, clear table surfaces and appropriate chairs will help your child with sitting skills and seated activities. Some children are as idiosyncratic in their choice of a chair as in other areas. They may prefer a chair with arms or one wedged into a corner of the room so that they feel safe and are less likely to escape. Even such apparently minor matters can help control undesirable behaviour, such as throwing objects or jumping up from the table at mealtimes. Some families may also need to organize eating implements – for example, using plastic plates or securing items to the table with Velcro if a child habitually throws these things.

If your child is a climber, it may be helpful to move furniture away from shelves or places that offer an easily accessible ledge. If she's a 'sweeper', keep shelves and tabletops clear and put ornaments and books out of reach on high shelves.

Some parents have found labels helpful. These can be pictures, photos or words. Labels on items such as drawers, bins and cupboards may help a child understand her environment better. Then, she may be more likely to use things for their intended purpose and less likely to indulge in inappropriate behaviour. For example, a visual label on the bin may help your child understand that this is a place for things that are no longer wanted, not an item to be tipped out and the contents rifled through. Others have found that coloured tape or material is useful for showing the child no go areas, such as the front hall or the cooker. Alternatively, simple 'Stop' signs can be put on doors, cupboards, drawers and so on.

Once your child has a better understanding of the environment and safety, you may be able to phase out some of these physical pointers. Meanwhile, they can only help a child learn important safety information and sociable behaviour, as well as keeping her out of harm's way.

Safety in the home

Unfortunately, children with autism may not outgrow the need for the kinds of home safety precautions most parents find necessary for toddlers. This is because autistic children often simply do not understand danger. They may have a compulsive curiosity about how things work and, at the same time, an overriding lack of awareness of dangerous situations, such as exploring the vacuum cleaner while it is still plugged in.

In general, you may need to child-proof the house as you would for a much younger child, with stair gates, plug covers and safety covers for ovens. Here are some more ideas.

- Use locks where appropriate. For children given to running away from home (see Elopement below), you may have to add higher-level locks on the front door. You may also want to add locks to certain rooms, such as the utility room housing the washing machine or the door of another child's room.
- Consider fitting safety locks to cupboard doors containing items such as food, medicines, cleaning materials, sharp knives, matches and so on. Window locks and safety glass are other options. Some parents have also had to place strips of wood across windows.
- Make sure that all electric wiring and preferably sockets, too, are hidden so that your child cannot play with the wires.
- Be aware of fire safety, keeping all lighters and matches out of reach, and supervise your child closely when there is an open fire or barbeque.
- Consider putting a non-slip mat in the bath and ensure that all cleaning products are out of reach. Using shampoos with a pump top may be an idea, instead of the screw-top ones.

Elopement

This quaint term is used to refer to children with autism who leave home, regularly walking out of the front door without telling anyone or whipping across several back gardens before the parents even realize that they have gone.

Giving your child an ID bracelet or necklace is an idea, if he or she will tolerate it, as autistic children are not always able to communicate where they live once they are out and about. Another option is to iron or sew labels into all the child's clothes. Some children can be taught to carry and show an identification card.

9

Behaviour and discipline

Discipline is a sore point for many parents of autistic children. They lose count of the times members of the public blame them for 'poor discipline' after their child has displayed behaviour that is less than desirable. Bad behaviour, such as tantrums, is deeply draining and upsetting, but you may find that 'normal' forms of discipline have little or no effect on your autistic child.

While he may need limits and guidelines even more than other children, laying them down may involve more than normal strength, clarity and tact. The firm setting of boundaries by you is worthwhile, however, as it is one of the factors that may help him feel safe, even if his own world feels out of control. While he may come to appreciate a structured and predictable world, it cannot all be on his terms. Your child needs to be part of your family, but without making your entire family life revolve around him, especially when there are other children in the family.

Much has been written by people with autism, letting the wider world know that autism is not a horrible tragedy and a 'cure' may be neither necessary nor desirable. This may be so, but from the viewpoint of 'neurotypicals', what is commonly viewed as 'bad' behaviour may need to be dealt with in order to protect the child and those around her.

As with all children, dealing with potentially difficult behaviour early can make all the difference in terms of how your child behaves later. It may not always work, however. Also, it can be very difficult for parents of autistic children to put into practice as they may have more temptations than most to go for the easier option and let their children get away with bad behaviour so as to maintain a little peace and happiness in the home. This is especially true if parents believe that this behaviour is 'just a phase' and that their child is a 'late bloomer'. Their intuition or feel for what is normal, allowable behaviour in a child becomes suppressed. What often happens is that, instead of the child being taught normal, socially accepted behaviour, the entire family accommodates the child and so learns abnormal behaviour as they bend over backwards to try and prevent temper tantrums and other bad behaviour. Like other children, your autistic child may use bad behaviour as a way to get your attention.

Typical mistakes include letting children run around with food because they refuse to sit at the table, allowing children to carry too many toys everywhere they go in order to pacify them, letting them hold their bottles or dummies all the time or allowing them to eat only certain foods or consistencies of foods.

Obviously, this is not fair on parents, other siblings or, indeed, the autistic child concerned. Sadly, too, giving in doesn't work – it only postpones bad behaviour or tantrums and teaches the child that such a level of behaviour is tolerable.

But . . .

This raises an important point. How teachable is your child? A child needs to be able to understand that he or she has done wrong in your eyes, otherwise any discipline will be beside the point. Autistic children may simply not understand why they shouldn't empty the washing powder all over the floor or eat the dog food or throw a wobbly in the supermarket. It can be a very tricky process to differentiate problem behaviour from that which comes about just because the child is in his own world. Often a child with autism is not intentionally annoying you or anyone else – he may be incapable of manipulation because he lacks the ability to empathize.

Inappropriate discipline is likely to do nothing to help a child understand the situation and why it was wrong to do what she did. Neither will it help prevent the situation from happening again in the future.

It is worth trying to look at the source of your child's behaviour before applying discipline to ensure that her 'misbehaviour' was nothing to do with an inability to manage and integrate her senses and her world.

In the end, remember that you know your child best – when he or she is genuinely distressed and when he or she is playing up – so you can take appropriate action. To be effective, any discipline needs to be individual, to fit the child like a glove, and take into account her mental and neurological state. For example, a child with autism who also suffers from seizures may not always be able to manage self-control by means of sheer willpower because of these neurological events or brainwave activity. Even at the best of times, a child's response to discipline may be uneven. For some parents, management may have to include protective devices, security measures and medication.

Typical behaviour

Tantrums are a particular feature of autism and controlling them may be important for more substantial reasons than simply wanting to avoid social embarrassment if, like many autistic children, yours is impervious to danger, perhaps given to jumping out of high windows or running into the street.

Tantrums in an autistic child may occur for reasons other than those causing typical toddler tantrums in that they may be a result of the sensory overload that is a typical feature of autism (see Sensory overload, below).

Another problem can be the child who escapes the house at every possible opportunity (Elopement, see Chapter 8). This can cause parents to lock all windows and doors and watch their child like a hawk all day.

Aggressive behaviour can be another distressing aspect of autistic disorders.

Sensory overload and behaviour

Children with autism may have a dysfunctional sensory system due to neurological problems in which one or more senses either over- or underreacts to stimulation. Such sensory problems may be the underlying reason for such behaviour as rocking, spinning and hand flapping. So, with bad behaviour, it may help to look closer for hidden causes. It may be that your disobedient, screeching child is simply doing so in response to stress. Unfortunately, what constitutes a stressor for your child may not be obvious and involve some detective work before it is discovered. Things that the average person barely notices can be major sources of fear and anxiety for your child, such as bright lights or crowds.

Bear in mind that, because of sensory differences, your child may see, touch and hear the world differently to you. As the famous autistic professor Temple Grandin puts it, 'The autistic child withdraws because the world is a hurtful place – sound hurts, touch hurts, vision hurts, everything hurts.'

Your child may learn skills to deal with overstimulation himself as he grows older, but for now he may need your help. He will need you to foresee when enough is enough, by limiting input and experiences, and by helping him regain calm and control after an outburst.

Professor Grandin, who has written widely on autism (see the Further reading section at the back of the book), relates the distress and relief of her sensory experiences in her book *Emergence: Labeled autistic*. She designed and created her own 'squeeze machine' or 'hug box'. This allowed her to deliver as much physical pressure as she desired to help calm her nervous system, the all-important part being that she retained control of it.

Professor Grandin reports that many children, especially if they are non-verbal, seek pressure as a comforter. You might find them wrapping themselves in blankets even when it is really hot or even lying between the mattress and the bed base. She recommends inexpensive ways to provide deep pressure, such as gym mats and beanbag chairs.

Born with sensory problems due to cerebellar abnormalities herself, Grandin speculates that secondary neurological damage and some behaviour problems could be made worse by withdrawal from touching. Given that the limbic system does not fully mature until two years after birth, Grandin suggests that, if children withdraw due to sensory or other problems, maybe these parts of their brains will not develop fully. Her theory is backed up by animal experiments. For example, some of the stereotypical behaviour exhibited by autistic children is also found in zoo animals that were raised from birth in a barren environment.

It may take a process of trial and error to find out just how much sensory stimulus each child can take and what their particular dislikes are. Forcing children into contact – for example, by making them maintain eye contact – may cause sensory overload and lead them to shut down, according to Professor Grandin, but neither can you leave these children shut up in their own world. The key lies in finding the right balance and keeping these children engaged with the world, but on their terms.

Professor Grandin suggests helpful ways in which to coax children into contact. For example, whispering in a room free of visual distractions or singing in a low, soft voice or very gently stroking those who pull away so that they become accustomed to touch little by little.

Managing your child's behaviour

This is certainly easier said than done! With practice, though, it may be possible to spot the signs of overload building up and so intervene well before a crisis point is reached. Obviously, you don't want your entire life to revolve around your child's moods and needs, but being aware of the warning signs can help to prevent some family discomfort.

Your child may well have some consistent ways of communicating stress, unhappiness or growing anger, either with certain forms of behaviour or perhaps by sounds or movements if not words. Once you have identified the signals that lead up to an outburst of rage or some other form of undesirable behaviour, it may be easier to take pre-emptive action, such as distraction – some children are easily redirected into a favourite, soothing activity.

Leo, four, loved shredding paper and this was his safety valve when a tantrum threatened. His mother Carol kept a box full of paper to be used as needed.

Mara had an old-fashioned spinning top that acted as a soother. She would press the knob down again and again and watch fascinated as the bright metal revolved.

Using relaxation techniques with your child is another option, such as music or deep breathing, if possible. Having a safe place, right away from any sensory stimulation, is an often recommended remedy for children on a bad day or after a tantrum.

Six-year-old Billie's parents tried to teach her deep breathing, but with little success – she couldn't bear them placing a hand on her abdomen to demonstrate just where she should breathe in. She did, however, enjoy going behind the sofa, to her own safe zone. It was curtained off and filled with cushions and she liked listening to the same CD (a times tables one) each time.

Like all children, your child may need a good bout of exercise before he or she can calm down (see also Chapter 8).

Obviously, it is best not to wait until your child is showing signs of stress before trying any of these ideas. Regular exercise and relaxation can be built into daily life to help make him or her more comfortable all round.

Finally, don't be afraid to take control – it can be reassuring. More than with other children, though, verbal tellings off need to be worded quite carefully if they're to serve any other purpose than relieving your stress. Children with autism seem to process any new information better – including behaviour management techniques – when it is given to them in clear, bite-sized pieces. Commands need to be precise, simple and concrete – a simple 'No!', for example. If the worst happens, try the following:

- ignore the bad behaviour for a minute or two, then try to redirect the child to some favourite activity
- give a simple, firm command, such as 'No' or 'Stop . . .' (be specific about what you want to stop, such as 'No kicking') and repeat it two or three times
- give specific commands to tell a child what to do instead – such as 'Feet still, feet down' after kicking
- reinforce any good behaviour with short, repeated expressions of praise – such as, 'Good girl, nice still feet'
- ask your child to leave the room if the behaviour persists
- bear in mind that your child may need to be told more than once.

Reward and discipline

Most children, either with or without autism, respond better if their good points are acknowledged and they are motivated and encouraged rather than just told what they are doing wrong. So try to reinforce good behaviour by praising it. As with all communication, keep what you say short and simple and repeat it a few times, at intervals, so that your child has a chance to take the words in. Think in terms of step-by-step reinforcement, making progress a little at a time, rather than in one giant stride. There is, of course, a difference between rewarding the right behaviour and offering a bribe to achieve the desired result!

Ignoring the bad behaviour is a good option, but may not always be possible. If you are reprimanding a child, try to focus on the specific behaviour, not the child, saying, for example, 'Hitting people is wrong', rather than, 'You're a naughty boy.'

Try to teach basic disciplinary skills that will make your child's life easier. An example might be the 'sitting skills' needed for school, which may be no more than being able to sit at the table for a meal with the rest of the family. It can be helpful to create schedules or timetables of daily duties, such as brushing teeth or dressing.

Ensure that you acknowledge any successes, however small, with praise.

Any discipline should be administered at once as delay may confuse the child. Ideally, it should mirror the crime as closely as possible. For example, if your child throws a bowl of cereal across the room, the punishment would be to clean it up and not have another bowlful, rather than just being sent to his or her room. Older children may understand having privileges withdrawn or time out or having to do extra jobs around the house.

Bad behaviour such as screaming or aggression may be due to frustration and the simple inability to express emotions of fear or unhappiness in what we consider to be the appropriate way. Teaching alternative communication skills may help, such as drawing pictures, especially if you show your child how to do these first, or acting or miming feelings.

Irritating behaviour

It does no one any harm, but what do you do when your child has mannerisms that you find desperately irritating? Echolalia, repetitive play activities, weird noises, constant humming, hand flapping – these types of behaviour are harmless in themselves, but, repeated day after day, can be extremely trying.

Bear in mind that these kinds of activities may be coping mechanisms for your child that help release or reduce stress. Thus, it may be helpful to assess your child's life overall for causes of stress and try to reduce them. Another reason might be that your child needs such to explore his or her own world of sensation due to the sensory differences between an autistic child's experience and that of a 'normal' child.

Exercises such as yoga, stretching and swimming might help to reduce some of the bizarre posturings and movements. Some research has shown that stress can contribute to some of the abnormal postures of autistic children and others have found that some children may have awkward postures as a result of general postural immaturity. As with bad behaviour, it may help to try and reduce the incidence of such activities rather than do away with them altogether. For example, if possible, they could be forbidden at table or on outings.

When you can't change it
Despite your best efforts, the behaviour won't change. Here are some ideas you can try:

- to deal with your reaction rather than the behaviour – go into another room and close the door, have a bath, turn the radio on or listen to a personal stereo with your headphones, get earplugs
- to take as much time out as you can – badger your friends, ask your partner, pester support agencies
- to change the situation so that you can bypass the annoying behaviour – for example, if your child's eating habits leave something to be desired, plan two meals, with an earlier one for children and a later one for adults.

Are you agreed?

A common problem is that parents have different expectations regarding behaviour and discipline – indeed, this happens in all families. For example, one parent lets a behaviour go, while the other is hugely annoyed by it and eventually blows up.

Tony was the soft touch with the children and enjoyed spending three days a week with them as he worked from home. His partner Bea, who had a high-pressured job four days a week, was much tougher and expected certain standards of behaviour from all three of their children, the eldest of whom, Oliver, was autistic.

Tony and Bea decided to draw up a clear agreement as to what they thought was acceptable behaviour from all their children, bearing in mind Oliver's capabilities. They also agreed on giving parental time out to each other when either of them felt the need – that is, if either of them felt that they were losing control during a bout of problem behaviour, they were free to call the other in for support or to hand over completely while they took a short break.

10
Stress and your feelings

Having a child with autism is notoriously challenging. It is vital for parents and other family members to have some time to themselves, see friends and so on despite all the extra work an autistic child can involve. This is because, as research suggests, parents of children with autism experience greater stress than those of children with mental retardation and Down's syndrome. The never-ending grind of care and consequent physical and mental exhaustion, lack of support, lack of personal freedom – the sources of this stress are many. There's also the children's inability to express their most basic needs, which can cause extraordinary frustration for both parents and children. Resulting from this frustration, there may be aggressive behaviour that threatens the parents, other siblings or the children themselves.

Other features of autism are also highly stressful, such as any repetitive, compulsive or unusual behaviour, sleeping problems and eating fads. The children's lack of social skills, such as appropriate play, may mean that they need to have their time constantly structured – a draining task and often not even possible at home. The children's behaviour may also prevent families from attending events together because one parent always has to babysit.

All of these things are both physically exhausting and emotionally draining. Having said all this, it is important to point out that families find many different ways of surviving. Some are saved by a robust sense of humour. Others manage to arrange work and activities outside the home in order to keep a healthy sense of perspective. For some, it's a question of just hanging on in there until it gets better. Bella's mother, Nina, puts it like this:

It's a question of watching the tiny bits of progress and accepting and loving your child for what she is. For long periods of time it seems as if all your work and help, all the love, all the support you get from others, is all going nowhere. But suddenly the child makes a leap forward and you realize that she was taking it all in, all the time – just waiting for the confidence and the right moment to show her progress. It's the small signs of growth and change that keep us going. We celebrate those.

Problems you may have

Autism impacts families in different ways, but it can affect your relationships and lifestyle to a profound degree, adding to an already stressful situation. Common problems include:

- differences with your partner regarding discipline
- inability to handle problem behaviour
- withdrawal by one parent or by one or more siblings or overinvolvement
- exhaustion or burnout
- resentment and blame (this latter can involve blaming each other for a child's poor genetic heritage)
- breakdown of extended family relationships
- increased distance from family, friends and community
- financial problems caused by having a child who needs extra attention
- problems with other children – sibling rivalry and so on.

It is important to stress that these problems are not unique to families with an autistic child. Money worries, the breakdown of relationships with the extended family and disagreements with partners can happen in any family.

Coming to terms with your feelings

Learning that your child is autistic is traumatic for parents, who feel that they have effectively 'lost' a child. Parents often move through the emotional stages of grief – denial, anger, bargaining, depression and, finally, acceptance. You need to give yourself permission and time to grieve, not just for the child you thought you were going to have, but also for the parents you thought you were going to be. Such images go very deep, right back to our own childhoods and upbringing.

You may also need to grieve for the loss of the lifestyle that you expected for your family. Many parents also mourn that their child may never engage in 'normal' activities, such as sport or attain some of life's milestones, such as a good education or marriage – what amounts to their child's unlived life.

79

However, this grief for a fantasy 'normal' child does need to be separated from the autistic child who is very much there and who, however poorly he expresses it, does need adult care and support as much as any child. Projecting grief on to the child prevents a relationship developing. Try to think of it in terms of grief for shattered expectations rather than for autism itself (see Chronic sorrow, below).

Chronic sorrow

Classically, the worst of the grief is 'supposed' to last for a year. With time, many parents come to accept their feelings and focus on helping their children to achieve what they can, finding joy and pride in the child as they adjust to what she is and what she can do.

Some people, however, experience ongoing grief, which is another stressor. Some research into grief suggests that parents of children with developmental disabilities continue to experience episodes of grief, triggered by life events such as birthdays, anniversaries and holidays. This makes for a kind of 'chronic sorrow' – a term coined by sociologist Simon Olshanshy to describe the long-term reaction of parents to having a child with a disability. He defined chronic sorrow as grieving without finality.

Many factors can affect chronic sorrow, such as your personality, how severely your child is affected and the type of support you have.

Experiencing chronic sorrow does not mean that you don't love your child. What it does mean is that the joy and pride of parenthood is mingled with this kind of ongoing grief for an indefinite period of time – sometimes for years. Chronic sorrow may even become a permanent part of your personality, perhaps transmuting into a more generalized awareness of the fragility of life and its potential griefs. It becomes a part of life, though not the ruling force – with most children there is usually far too much to do and too much love to give to allow grief to dominate.

View of a person with autism

Grief for a 'lost' child needs to be differentiated from reactions to autism. While non-autistic people may view autism as a tragedy, this may not always be the case, according to some people with autistic disorders. Not only do those with autism have their own ways of viewing life, they also need to be accepted and loved for who they are:

Autism is not a condition but a way of being ... there's no normal child hidden behind the autism. Autism is a way of being. It is pervasive; it colours every experience, every sensation, perception, thought, emotion, and encounter, every aspect of existence. It is not possible to separate the autism from the person.

You try to relate to your autistic child, and the child doesn't respond. He doesn't see you; you can't reach her; there's no getting through.

That does not mean that the child is incapable of relating at all. It only means you're assuming a shared system, a shared understanding of signals and meanings, that the child in fact does not share. It's as if you tried to have an intimate conversation with someone who has no comprehension of your language. Autistic people are 'foreigners' in any society.

You didn't lose a child to autism. You lost a child because the child you waited for never came into existence. That isn't the fault of the autistic child who does exist, and it shouldn't be our burden. We need and deserve families who can see us and value us for ourselves, not families whose vision of us is obscured by the ghosts of children who never lived. Grieve if you must, for your own lost dreams. But don't mourn for us. We are alive. We are real. And we're here waiting for you ... We need you. We need your help and your understanding. Your world is not very open to us, and we won't make it without your strong support.

Just because someone cannot speak, doesn't mean they have nothing to say ... listen and look and love.

'Don't Mourn for Us' by Jim Sinclair, founder of Autism Network International, an autistic-run self-help organization for those with autism – a speech that he gave at the 1993 International Conference on Autism in Toronto.

Grieving is a stressful, tiring process that takes time. During this time you may need to be alone or turn away from the friends who have supported you until now and seek the company of other grievers. Being part of a support group or receiving professional counselling may help you and your family to accept the diagnosis, move forwards and learn how to best help your child develop to his greatest potential.

Ensure early intervention

This advice has been given before in this book, but it is definitely worth repeating here because of the often horrific struggles so many parents go through before their child is diagnosed and receives help. The process can take years and this certainly adds to the stress.

A diagnosis does end doubt and, while this may involve grief, as we have seen above, it cuts down on the stress caused by the previous uncertainty. On a practical level, it also means that you can start the vital process of petitioning for extra care and educational help for your child. Not only does this take some of the physical burden off you – knowing that the best is being done for your child – it also reduces stress. This is the time when, if you haven't done so before, it is well worth joining a good support group, such as the National Autistic Society (NAS) in the UK or the Autism Society of America, as they provide information and support as you go through this difficult process.

Having a break and taking time out for yourself

A life that wholly revolves around an autistic child is the all too common lot of many parents. However, it is really important to remember that there is life beyond autism. It is vital to make time for yourself to keep sane, healthy and avoid burnout. The classic response to this advice is 'No time', but bear in mind that even a few minutes a day can make a difference. So can very simple things, such as making yourself a favourite snack or applying hand lotion. Parents also need to give themselves rewards to keep their motivation going and energy levels up, especially given the extra frustration and stress that goes with bringing up a child with autism.

Family members need to reward – that is, acknowledge – one another. For example, tell your partner that you really appreciated the break while he took the children out to the park – don't just take it for granted.

It is important, too, to try and spend some time alone with your partner, even if it's just watching television together or going out for lunch while the children are at school. It doesn't have to last for hours – quality is more important than quantity.

It might help to spend a few minutes consciously setting your priorities apart from autism. After all, autism is not what originally brought you and your partner together or influenced earlier life decisions. Such priorities might relate to areas of your life such as the following:

- your own personal belief structure or value system
- your partner
- your other children
- extended family
- work
- hobbies and interests
- community involvements and any other obligations.

Planning for your child's future

One of the most significant sources of stress for parents is anxiety about their child's future care. Parents know that they provide their child with exceptional care and fear that no one will take care of their child in the same way if they become ill or too old to do the job. A difficult task to bequeath at the best of times, it is one that may be impossible for other family members to take on.

It is important to get these concerns out into the open and make a plan. Some parents draw up a contract with a professional guardian who agrees to look after the interests of the person with autism, such as observing birthdays and arranging for care (see also Chapter 12).

Planning your finances

Having a child with autism can drain a family's monetary as well as other resources. Apart from extra medical or treatment expenses, one parent might only be able to do less well paid jobs or have to give up work altogether because of the demands of caring for their child.

Support

What kind of support system you have makes a huge difference to how well you cope with an autistic child and how well you feel in yourself. Unfortunately, other people can be a source of stress and upset. Due to social discomfort, there is sometimes pressure on parents to finish with or hide any grief or negativity they feel. You may be told to 'think positively' and 'get on with your life'. Perhaps most galling of all is the suggestion that God has 'chosen' you to receive this special child because you are such a strong person or because the spiritual gifts to be gained from this commitment are so tremendous. This may well be so, but it may not be what you want to hear as you are reeling from the diagnosis or struggling to change the nappy of a hefty, howling three-year-old or trying to halt yet another public tantrum.These kinds of well-meant comments deny your feelings of grief, discomfort and rage, as well as your very real difficulties. They are also very isolating.

You may well find that you need to augment your support system or create a new one with the help of an autism support group. Two excellent ones are the National Autistic Society (NAS) in the UK and the Autism Society of America. As well as being a potential source of new, caring friends, such organizations can provide practical advice and information on the latest research, as well as suggestions on how to access care for your child and financial support. You are not alone.

Some parents also find it satisfying to contribute to greater awareness of autism, perhaps by working for further resources, community programmes or school services. Knowing that you are helping others with autism is a source of strength for many.

Finding the support you need to help care for your child is also important, including respite care, and this is covered more fully in Chapter 12, Help.

Other ways to reduce stress

There are many ways you can try to reduce stress – most of which mean making just a few minutes for yourself. They include exercise, meditation and prayer, breathing and relaxation exercises and keeping a diary. If you are feeling overwhelmed by the demands of your autistic child and other difficulties, counselling is a very valuable option to consider. Just talking to someone can help you to clarify areas of confusion and set priorities.

Finally, access help – any help going, from Social Services, friends or other agencies. Even if it takes the last scrap of energy you have left and waiting lists, paperwork and bureaucracy leave you exasperated, it is worth it in the long run (see also Chapter 12, Help).

Dealing with social isolation and misunderstanding

Taking an autistic child out can be highly stressful for parents in the face of public misunderstanding (or complete lack of understanding) of the disorder. Children who throw tantrums, walk on their toes, flap their hands, steal strangers' food or rifle through their bags can be highly embarrassing. As the disorder is invisible, many people react to autistic children and their parents in a less than friendly way, because they mistakenly think that the child is just incredibly badly behaved. They may stare or openly comment, perhaps blaming the child or you for lack of discipline and 'letting them get away with it'.

Sal's mother, Miranda, found that once she gave the simple explanation, 'I'm sorry, my child has autism', things were easier and people were more accepting. 'The most difficult challenge for my family is dealing with ignorance', she added.

Even if nothing happens, you may start dreading outings or feel uncomfortable taking your child to the homes of friends or relatives. This makes holidays an especially difficult time for families. Feeling that you can't easily visit friends or socialize because of your child's behaviour and that your experiences are so different to those of others, it is quite easy to start feeling isolated from friends, family and the wider community. It is important, though, however hard it may be, to beat those feelings down and get on with it. Your autistic child doesn't learn anything by just staying at home day in day out and you need to get out, too. Also, some people are incredibly helpful and positive.

Some autistic children will pick up on tensions in the family or those watching and predictably rise to the occasion with a display of their worst behaviour. However, as Miranda says:

Once you have given a simple explanation, you don't owe

85

anybody anything. If others then understand, the problem is solved. If they don't understand and walk away, even with a judgmental attitude, the problem is still solved – it is their problem and not mine.

Holidays

Holidays are a mixed blessing for the parents of autistic children and can develop into downright trials. While it may be lovely to have a break from the school run and plan picnics and outings, holidays are also a potential source of stress. Will your autistic child have an accident? Can you keep him busy enough? What about keeping his brothers and sisters happy?

- Realize that you cannot duplicate the school's routine. A family is more fluid and unpredictable and your autistic child has, to a certain extent, to learn to fit in with this – it may even do him good.
- Don't ignore brothers and sisters while you try to fit in therapies and treatments for your autistic child. Find a babysitter, ask relatives or friends to stay with your child and take your other children out, too. Above all, don't feel guilty.
- Have a rota for whoever is in charge of watching the autistic child at family get-togethers, picnics or other outings, such as friends and babysitters (try to leave siblings out of such duties). This will free the rest of the family to enjoy holiday events.
- If your child will accept it, an ID bracelet for them can help reduce anxiety about what will happen if they wander off.
- Bring any food your child requires. To avoid embarrassment in group situations, you could simply say that many foods interact negatively with your child's medication.
- The long summer holidays present a good opportunity for parents to try out therapies and treatments that can't be fitted into term time, such as music or art therapy. Don't try to cram too much in, though – everyone will end up exhausted! Try one this summer and see how it goes – preferably choosing ones that you have word of mouth recommendations for.

Families need support

Families of children with autism are not getting the support they need, according to a report from the national charity Shared Care Network. The report showed an urgent need to increase short respite breaks for such families. One in three children with disabilities on waiting lists for short breaks has autism.

The report looked at nearly 300 families of children and teenagers with autistic spectrum disorders and showed that parents of children with autism suffer from stress and exhaustion.

Of the families questioned, 82 per cent said that they needed to supervise their child 24 hours a day. They said that their child's condition was often misunderstood and more than half received no regular help from friends and family.

Short break services were shown to help families cope by giving parents a respite from caring. They also gave children with autism the chance to meet new people and gain new experiences.

11
Family and friends

Having an autistic child in the family can bring out the very best in other family members, developing in young children a maturity and depth of understanding well beyond their years. Many of them regard their 'different' brother or sister as special and precious. As psychologist Judy Dunn points out, 'The intimacy and emotional power of this relationship can foster remarkable capabilities in . . . young children.' However, on a day-to-day, nitty-gritty basis, there can be difficulties. How do you make time for brothers and sisters? How do you stop the quarrels? Then there's the wider, extended family as well as friends. Do they really understand? How do you explain to your own parents that your child is not the grandchild of their dreams?

It is important to keep things in perspective and remember that 'normal' family life is by no means perfect either. Most families have their share of quarrels, jealousy and bad temper. The same applies to grandparents, the extended family and friends. Not all grandparents react to a grandchild in ways you might expect. Many live their own lives and don't make as much time for your children as you may have anticipated. Friendships, too, change and sometimes cool when one couple has children and the other doesn't or if you move. You may simply grow away from each other. While an autistic child may add to family difficulties, he or she is unlikely to be the sole cause of them.

Will my other children suffer?

Parents can worry that their other children may be at risk of developing problems because of the autistic child's social and behaviour problems. Research has suggested that, although living with an autistic sibling can be a stressful experience at times, far from being harmed by their experiences, the siblings are often remarkably well-adjusted and more mature and responsible than their peers, feel more positive about themselves and generally more selfless and tolerant. The effects of having an autistic sibling do vary from family to family, however. Some studies of families with an autistic child have reported higher rates of behaviour problems in their siblings than in the control groups studied, while others have found few major differences between the two groups, though the autistic children themselves often reported more feelings of anxiety and being neglected than the other children.

How parents handle the issue can make a great difference. One of the major factors in a positive outcome appears to be that there is open discussion with the other children – of what is going on, the nature of the problem and what is likely to happen in the future. This eliminates much anxiety and confusion before it even has a chance to start to develop (see under the heading Open discussion – keeping other siblings informed, below). Problems with siblings may be greater if:

- the family is small, with just two children and a small age gap between them, as in larger families, the burden is more easily shared, the autistic child finding his or her own level among the other siblings and parents' attention is spread more evenly – they cannot focus so strongly on their anxiety and grief regarding the autistic child
- the sibling is younger than the child with autism as he or she may miss out on parental attention
- the problem with the autistic child is severe
- there are other negative factors – poor family relationships, financial strains, friction between the parents, depression or illness in the parents and so on as all these things increase the risk of problems.

One of the most powerful influences on siblings' adjustment appears to be how positive the parents' attitude is. Several studies have shown that, providing the burden of care is not too great, acceptance and positive attitudes in parents are mirrored in their other children.

Siblings and learning problems

While this is an upsetting issue for parents, it is important to be aware of possible risks to the other children, particularly in terms of problems with language-related or learning skills.

Looking for the good points
Part of being positive involves encouraging your children to see the good side of your autistic child – this is very important. Fortunately, these good points don't have to be earth-shattering, as research by Judy Dunn shows. She describes one seven-year-old boy who disliked being separated from his affected brother 'because I miss him snoring, which stops me having bad dreams'!

Some studies have shown an increased risk of language, speech and developmental problems in the other children in families with an autistic child. For example, learning problems, speech delays or reading and spelling later than average. Like autism, this probably has a genetic component. To put this another way, families that have a genetic predisposition for communication or learning problems will not necessarily develop autism, though autism is one of a number of possible outcomes for children with this genetic makeup.

It is possible for such problems to be overlooked because the family focus is on the autistic child. Parents may also blame the difficulties on the pressures of living with an autistic sibling – having less time than they would like to spend with the other child or children and so on. In some instances this may be the case, but it is important to take any problems a child is having seriously in their own right and to ensure that help and treatment, if necessary, are made available from the earliest stages. This is important as even relatively mild problems of language development and with reading or spelling can affect your child's social and academic development.

Personal and social problems your other children may have

The severe disruption caused to family life is the most noticeable problem your child is likely to have.

Cara, 13, sister of Jack, who is 5, notes:

Lack of privacy. Never being able to leave personal belongings around, having to keep my bedroom door locked all the time, being careful not to put homework down and forget it while you go to the loo. Not really being able to plan normal family outings, being embarrassed to have friends round unless you're barricaded into the bedroom. That's the downside of having an autistic sibling.

Some children feel that family life revolves around the autistic member and so they receive less attention. They may also suffer frustration at not being able to get a response from their brother or sister and may be the target of aggressive outbursts.

They may feel the burden of care – for example, being expected to do more housework or be more mature than their affected sibling. Interestingly, however, some studies have shown that concerns about excessive housework are no greater in children in these families than they are in their peers! One study also found that a disabled child in the family very much increases the amount of work to be done in the home and, surprise, surprise, almost all of this was done by their mothers.

In particular, older children may feel more psychological stress in such families. For example, feeling that they have to achieve excellent results at school, support their parents emotionally and, perhaps, prepare to support their sibling financially, too, in later life if their parents die.

Other concerns may be subtler and can include identity problems. An example would be the normal child who perhaps has secret fears that he or she might also be affected by autism in some way. Some children can feel guilt or fear that they might have caused the condition or else will be tarred with the same brush in the eyes of others.

Socially, while studies indicate that, in the long term, a child's social world is not likely to be affected, there can be problems such as ignorance or teasing from other children.

What you can do

There are several actions you as parents can take to help family life run more smoothly. What you do will, of course, depend on how severely your autistic child is affected by their condition. Many of the following suggestions are common sense, but can be forgotten in

How siblings may react at different ages

Preschool children

Under-fives are more likely to show their feelings via their behaviour than in what they say. They will be unable to understand the special needs of their sibling, but they will notice differences and try to teach their brother or sister. Children of this age are likely to enjoy their sibling because they have not learned to be judgmental.

Primary school age (6–12)

As your child ventures out more into the world, he may become more aware of the differences between people. He may need to be reassured about some of his sibling's puzzling or frightening behaviour. He can now understand a simple explanation of his sibling's special needs, such as 'Sam doesn't know how to talk.'

He may worry that the disability is contagious or if something is wrong with him, too. He may have conflicting feelings about his brother or sister (this happens in 'normal' families, too), as well as guilt for having negative thoughts about his sibling or for being the child who is not disabled.

Some typical responses of children this age are to become either *too* good and helpful or disobedient in order to obtain a parent's attention. He may also need help with questions such as how to explain autism to his friends.

Adolescents (13–17)

Teenagers obviously will want more detailed explanations of autism, for example a conversation about the possible genetic basis of autism. Your teenager may be concerned about the future of the autistic child in terms of education, work, relationships and marriage – especially if they fear that they may in the future share responsibility for the child.

Some teenagers are particularly sensitive to peer pressure and may find their sibling embarrassing in front of boy or girl friends they want to impress. They want to maintain their relationship with the family, but need independence as well, which can result in conflict (again, this situation is not confined to families with an autistic child).

the day-to-day welter of tasks to be done, phone calls, shopping and so on. They include:

- open discussion – keeping other children informed
- making time for siblings
- meeting the social and educational needs of the other children
- involving your other children
- 'It's not fair' – are you treating them differently?

The next sections look at these points in more detail.

Open discussion – keeping other children informed

Open discussion with the whole family about the child with an autistic disorder seems to be a major factor in how well they understand and cope. It is a mistake to try to 'shield' them. Even very small children have insights to contribute and need a chance to express both their positive and negative feelings.

Your other children need to know what autism is and a bit about how it is diagnosed and treated, as well as what to expect and the nature of children with autism. Tailor information to your child's age – the younger the child, the briefer the explanation that is required, but be aware that their need for information will change with the years. Bear in mind, too, that children of all ages may repeat and use the words they hear without understanding their full meaning. Explanations need to be repeated and added to over the years.

Some children feel guilt that they have somehow caused the autism. An open discussion is invaluable as a means of airing such feelings. Even if they seem irrational to adults, they are all too real for the child. For example, in one study of autistic twins by Professor Ann Le Couteur of the University of Newcastle, one twin was convinced that her sister's autism had resulted from when she had hit her on the head with a book. Throughout her childhood she had been too terrified to tell anyone of her fears and had lived with this guilt for years.

Other children may feel guilt due to often ambivalent or negative feelings they have about their sibling and need to be reassured that such feelings are natural. They may also appreciate simple advice about ways in which they could handle day-to-day problems.

Open discussion can also help family members cope with stressful

93

events, such as dealings with friends' curiosity, reactions from the public, as well as coping with extra responsibilities at home and the future of their autistic brother and sister. As mentioned, this last point can cause a lot of anxiety. Older children will appreciate you making it plain that they have their own lives to lead.

Making time for siblings

Setting aside regular times for other children can be a great help. Obviously, this is not always easy and may mean that the autistic child has to receive less than perfect attention. Parents find different ways of fitting in the time – perhaps when their autistic child is returning home from a care centre or school, or when he is settled in bed. Others split the time between the two parents or share the job with grandparents, friends or babysitters.

Spending time together out of the house, without the autistic child, often works better – for example, on a hobby or extracurricular class or just having a snack out or going shopping. As Claire notes:

> Apart from anything else, being out together is one time when I am really listening to my other children and don't have half an ear open for what Sam may be doing. It's a time when we can really talk about them, what they're doing, their strengths and weaknesses and any problems. I have always made a point of Natasha and Josh doing classes and activities they enjoy – ballet and swimming, mostly. We really use that time. Sometimes we get Dad or a babysitter to start early and go out so we can sit in the car and chat for half an hour.
>
> The same applies to parents, I think – we need to spend time outside the home and do our own thing.

As the autistic child grows older, one of the best ways in which to spend time with the rest of the family is to demand respite care. Again, this is not always easy to find and many parents feel guilty about it, but it does offer everyone – including parents – the chance to recharge their batteries. Such care received on a regular basis will probably be accepted more easily by the autistic child than if it happens randomly (see also Chapter 12, Help).

Families may also want to go out together from time to time without the child with autism, for example to a film or amusement park. This may cause guilt, but everyone deserves to enjoy time together that is not threatened by the challenges of autism.

Meeting the social and educational needs of the other children

As your other children grow older they will need to engage in school and social as well as home life. You can help by ensuring privacy, so that your other children can entertain friends, keep their own possessions safe, and do homework – a simple lock on the bedroom door is effective.

Give them a chance to meet others in the same situation. There are several groups for siblings of autistic children and these provide them with a valuable chance to discuss feelings that may be difficult to express to the family and, most of all, to know that they are not the only ones going through this.

There are numerous resources explaining more about siblings' needs and experiences – books, newsletters and videos. For example, a chatroom for siblings of children with disabilities called 'SibChat' meets periodically. A final resource to consider, particularly for those who are experiencing difficulty in adapting to their sibling's disability, would be individual counselling.

Involving your other children

This can require finding a delicate balance. Your other children need to interact with and help their autistic sibling, but, naturally, don't want to be pressed into service all the time. Many feel that they have to give more physical and emotional support to parents than their peers, though these feelings may not always be justified. Girls appear more likely to be at risk of this than boys.

While you don't want to quash all altruistic feelings, outside interests need to be developed as much as possible, especially given the tendency of some children to become overinvolved.

Interestingly, several studies have shown that other siblings are often better at managing autistic children than parents, especially improving behaviour and increasing their skills, such as attending, obeying simple instructions and good play. One video study showed that children who learned these skills played together more and seemed much happier than they had been prior to training.

All this, apart from boosting siblings' self-esteem and making parents feel happier, is obviously important for the autistic child. Apart from anything else, he or she may not otherwise have the chance to interact so closely with other normal children.

In families with more able autistic children, the process does not have to be entirely one way. Your other children may also benefit

95

from the autistic child's special interest in, say, maths or history. In one family, for example, the older autistic brother is currently giving his 16-year-old sister extra coaching for her maths 'A' levels. In return, she is helping to desensitize him so he can overcome his dog phobia. Finally, it is important to remember to thank siblings for helping out with their brothers and sisters.

Warning signs

Having a child with autism can be a great strain on families at times. Many families have other sources of stress as well. Children vary in how they show any feelings of depression and stress. Signs that all may not be well with your other children include:

- depression
- irritability
- anxiety, perhaps about the health of other family members
- a change in the child's sleeping or eating habits
- seeming down, crying at small frustrations, feelings of hopelessness
- a child talks about hurting himself – for example, saying, 'I wish I was dead'
- difficulty with making decisions or concentrating
- lack of pleasure in activities
- social withdrawal
- school phobia
- somatic symptoms – stomach aches and headaches, for example.

If your child has several of these symptoms for two weeks or more, it may be advisable to consult your doctor.

'It's not fair' – are you treating them differently?

Seeing the autistic child 'get away with' bad behaviour is likely to rouse fury in the mildest of children. Obviously, some allowances do need to be made for the autistic child, but it is essential to explain the reasons for these to the other children. Also, that each child is special, including them, and so they cannot always be treated in exactly the same ways.

It helps to have certain rules of behaviour for the autistic child as well as the others and to ensure that these are kept to as far as possible so that there is a basic framework in place. It can also help if the autistic child is seen to help out with some routine chores, no matter how simple these may be, in the interests of equality.

Later on, in the case of more capable autistic children, the tables may be turned, with the autistic child complaining more about the unfairness of life than her siblings. For example, she may well resent not being allowed to do the same things or go to the same school or on the same outings as her brothers and sisters. Clearly, dealing with this situation requires considerable skill and sensitivity on the part of parents.

Other family and friends

At some time, most people feel the need to inform other family members of a diagnosis of autism.

This is likely to meet with a range of reactions – a simple lack of understanding, disbelief, denial or an inability to cope with the diagnosis because 'the child looks so normal'. It may be especially hard if you too did not notice anything was wrong for a while.

Claire remembers:

My parents and sister would sit and watch Sam to see if they could 'spot it', and ask me if I was sure the doctor had got it right. I know what they meant – it had taken us three years to suspect something might be amiss. Autism is not like an extra big toe. Its invisibility makes it harder on everyone, but people just don't realize that sleep problems, sensory sensitivities and social or emotional difficulties are classic symptoms of his autism – not signs of a child in need of more discipline.

Some family members may simply not want to talk about it. Others may admit that they had always suspected that something was wrong with the child, but never said anything, which can be hurtful – especially given that receiving help for the child early on is so vital.

It is important to bear in mind that your parents don't always live up to your expectations as grandparents, even with normal children. They're too busy, have lives of their own, no time to visit or babysit

97

or are plain disinterested. They don't play with the child when they visit or take her out. Many older men may not know what to do with a young child if they grew up in an era when men were less involved in the nitty-gritty care of an infant than is the case today. Some, too, dislike grandchildren as they are a reminder that they themselves are growing older. If, to cap it all, the grandchild turns out not to be 'normal' this can be the final straw in making grandparents turn their backs.

Other grandparents, like parents, can find that they need to grieve the loss of the 'normal' or 'typical' grandchild that they expected to have. In addition, grandparents are concerned about the stress and difficulties that they see their children experiencing. They may want to help, but don't know how. They may well lack expertise in the behaviour management skills needed for the child with autism – what worked for them when they were parents may simply cause frustration in their grandchild. Also, some grandparents may simply be physically unable to manage an autistic child. Perhaps saddest of all, some grandparents had just wanted to play with and spoil their grandchildren. Unfortunately, autism often prevents this dream from becoming a reality.

While friends often try to be supportive, they may not always understand the difficulties involved in raising an autistic child. They may criticize the parents for letting their child 'get away' with certain behaviour and announce how they would handle the child. It may be wearisome to repeat information about autism, but this is your best bet for encouraging acceptance.

Some parents of children with autism may feel sad or envious when seeing their friends' 'normal' children and their lives together. Some measure of drifting apart as a result of this and other differences may be inevitable, but doesn't have to be the case. On the other hand, many parents find that they get fantastic support and strength from new friends made via autism support groups.

12
Help

Getting help is often a highly stressful part of having a child with autism. All too often, families have to battle for financial support amid a tangle of bureaucracy, according to a report by the National Autistic Society.

The report also said that more than a third of carers did not understand the benefits system and almost two-thirds of those who had applied for benefits said that they had experienced problems filling out the forms. Many of the respondents who received benefits said that they had had to fight for them, with 30 per cent of those receiving Disability Living Allowance doing so as a result of an appeal. In addition, care provided by Social Services was described as being difficult to access, providing an unsatisfactory service and often not understanding families' needs. The specific needs of people with autism (social skills training and play and leisure facilities) were also often not being met.

Another report from the children's charity Barnardo's found that many families with a disabled child are still facing poverty because of the extra costs involved, such as specialist equipment and the fact that one of the parents often cannot work due to the demands of caring for the child.

These kinds of grim reports are becoming more common as autism agencies fight to increase awareness of autism. However, for parents who cannot wait for public and government attitudes to change, how can they get the help they desperately need?

Perhaps the first step is to admit, without guilt, just how much that help is needed. It is vital for parents to have breaks in order to recharge their batteries and gain the strength needed for the many demands they face in their daily lives.

The next step is to persist and make getting help a priority. It may be useful to look on it as a short-term job that has to be sorted out as a matter of urgency before your life can continue.

Support groups

Seek out local support groups, even if your child does not yet have an official diagnosis of autism. If he or she does, the earlier you inform yourself about it, the better the likely outcome for your child.

In the UK, the National Autistic Society (NAS) has groups throughout the UK and provides a very wide range of information and support for people with autism. This and other support groups can also give detailed advice on rights and benefits and how to access them.

Respite and residential care

Some parents feel very guilty when it comes to considering whether or not to let their child go away for a short break. Remember, while you may well need the time off in order to avoid burnout, there is growing recognition that a break may be good for your child, too – both in the short and long term. As well as bolstering her confidence and independence now, planned respite care means that if a crisis does arise in the future, your child has somewhere familiar to go. It can also pave the way for future residential care should it ever be needed.

In the UK, respite care is generally in short supply, but you can contact your local Social Services office for information on how to apply for it. A support group such as the NAS may also be able to provide details on how to proceed if you cannot access respite care.

Although it is rare, some parents will have to make the difficult decision to place their child in a residential school. When one child's needs overwhelm the family, parents may have to consider this option – both for the welfare of the autistic child, who may achieve greater independence in a safe environment, and for the rest of the family, who may finally be able to have a life.

June movingly describes how she made the hardest decision of her life: to let her seven-year-old son Alexander go into care because she could no longer cope. Years of destructive behaviour, including smearing the entire bedroom with faeces every day, had worn her and her husband down:

I was becoming increasingly desperate, because I just couldn't cope with the bizarre behaviour – the screaming fits when something wasn't as he wanted it and the round-the-clock vigil that was necessary to prevent him from escaping from the house and running into the road. He was phenomenally quick and would be past you if you took your eyes off him for a second, leaving a trail of destruction in his wake – smashed lights, curtains pulled from their hooks, to name but two of his favourite pastimes.

In the event, this was a positive decision as the home was able to toilet train Alexander and June was able to visit when she wanted.

Some parents who dislike the idea of putting their child into care may consciously, or unconsciously, be relying on other family members to help or to take over as caretakers. You do need to be very sure that this is indeed what they want to do. While it is important to involve others, such as grandparents and other children, in decisions and plans for your autistic child, it is vital that no one feels duty-bound to take over the child's care at some future point.

Other sources of help

In the UK, Social Services may be able to provide a range of other kinds of help, such as community care – a plan that considers various needs, such as accommodation, healthcare, education, home help, help with travel and holidays, funding and grants.

What Social Services don't provide is treatment. See the Useful addresses section at the back of the book for telephone and Internet contacts.

The NAS is developing a range of befriending schemes around the country. Such schemes involve volunteers helping to support the family and sometimes offering temporary respite.

In the UK, you may be able to claim benefits depending on how severe your child's autism is and your individual circumstances. The main benefits include those available as a result of the Carers and Disabled Children Act 2000, whereby councils can set up direct payments for parents or guardians of a disabled child (visit the website www.carers.gov.uk for more information) and the Disability Living Allowance (DLA). Find out more by contacting your local Social Services office, Post Office, ringing the Benefit Enquiry Line (0800 882200) or going to your local Citizens Advice Bureau.

Planning your child's long-term care

Although this is a task that many families understandably don't wish to face, it can relieve anxiety about the future to make a detailed, long-term plan for your child well before it becomes necessary. The aim is to make the transition from living at home to independent living as easy as possible, should you become ill or simply unable to care for your child any longer.

The following steps may help you start to organize your thoughts in the face of this daunting, sometimes seemingly overwhelming task. Try to find someone to help you, such as family or friends, your doctor or child's other carers, or consult professional help via governmental agencies, organizations or local support groups.

- **Draft a life plan** With family and friends if possible, decide what you want for your child in terms of residential needs, employment, education, social activities and medical care.
- **Write it down** Include information about, and contact details for, doctors, dentists, medicine, functioning abilities, types of activities enjoyed, daily living skills and rights and values.
- **Write down short, clear notes** or make a video of everyday activities, such as bathing, dressing, feeding, toileting, play and how your child communicates.
- **Consider legal issues** such as provision for the child in your will, trustees, guardians and who will manage money matters and benefits for your child, as well as care costs and other decisions.
- **Work out the cost** Calculate your monthly expenses and work out how much will be needed to provide enough funds to support his or her lifestyle. Don't forget to include disability income, social security benefits and so on.
- **Research resources** Possible resources to fund your plan include government benefits, family assistance, inheritances, savings, life insurance and investments.
- **Prepare legal documents** Choose a qualified lawyer to help you prepare wills, trusts, power of attorney, guardianship and so on.
- **Give copies of the relevant documents and instructions** to family and those involved in your child's care.
- **Review your plan** At least once a year, review and update the plan, modifying legal documents as necessary.

Even if you do not do all of the above, making a will with clear provision for your child can only give more peace of mind.

Conclusion

An autistic child mimics all the British traditionally hate most about children – impervious to discipline, demanding and antisocial. The dictum that children should be seen and not heard does not apply here. The UK has, time and again, been branded as a society where children are crowded out. The results of a survey of 2000 families in the UK by the magazine *Mother & Baby* clearly demonstrated that the vast majority of parents feel that the UK is child-unfriendly – dirty, unsafe and with inadequate facilities for them. Dogs' mess, vandalized playgrounds and cars speeding by all militate against the quality of family life. Many parents said that they felt unsafe walking their toddlers down the street. Many were turned away from restaurants because they had a baby. In a culture that values its young so little, you might almost say that to have a child at all is to be disabled. Further, from such a perspective, to have a disabled child is a tragedy, a total interruption of normal life as society knows, or dictates, it.

It is against a background of such a grudging culture where children are concerned, a creepy, Victorian prurience about children that pervades the UK's press, from the ghoulish accounts of child murders to the estimates of what a child 'costs' to bring up (anything from £10,000 to £100,000 depending on what you read), that the needs of autistic children are to be considered, and the needs of their parents. If a typical child prevents the making and spending of money and is a costly item in economic terms, how much more so must a child with special needs be?

There is tremendous pressure on parents to be normative, to 'cure' their 'problem' child so that he or she fits better into society. There is an entire ongoing social discourse that firmly marginalizes disabled children and their families. The emphasis is on fixing the problem or minimizing or managing it as far as possible – the so-called 'medical model of disability', as opposed to the 'social model of disability' which looks beyond a person's impairment to wider social forces that restrict people.

Of course, parents with an autistic child have to live somehow, control the breakages and the violent mood swings, the mess-making

103

and the screaming. This is what this book, in some small measure, has been about – how to manage as best you can in what are often appallingly difficult conditions. However, there is another face to managing the 'problem', the creation of a whole new subsociety in which social and personal expectations have to be relearned. The autistic child may not make a full contribution to society's economy; he or she may never work, and may be unlikely to mature into a consumer. A child of high ability may carve out her own niche at a senior professional level, but this may be on her terms, while she remains enclosed within a self-sufficient 'society' of her own.

Does this matter? Given the constraints and demands of society, it is perhaps surprising that there is not more autism than there is, that more people do not shut off (though this implies voluntary choice and such action may be beyond the autistic child's capabilities – he may do so from neurological necessity, rather than choice). Those with autism are never fully shut off, however. They are still communicative beings, even if this is just passive, as, without their carer's communications, from the basics of food and drink onwards, they would not survive. The tragedy is that society may be missing out on what autistic children have to offer.

Individual parents may emphatically not need autism to act as a spiritual wake-up call to their sense of values or humour. However, the metaphor of autism reminds society that all children are unfathomable – unique, unpredictable, unable to be pigeonholed, that they cannot always be treated as quantifiable objects, educated in the same ways or defined in monetary terms. Autism may also be a powerful metaphor for society's single-minded pursuit of economic values above all else, its disengagement from family, its pervasive dismissal of other states of mind, other cultural backgrounds – a way of being that has sinister implications for our present age. Autism is an interruption to the dominant belief in never-ending progress that underlies Western capitalism.

Taken too far, seeing autism as a cultural metaphor may be an affront to families who are having to deal with the reality of the condition every day. However, autism remains a reminder that some children, with their very different values and ways of being, may be here not to be cured, but to be loved and accepted as they are. This means taking their difficulties into account on their own terms, including the often acute sensory stresses that can make life so painful for them.

CONCLUSION

As Gail Gillingham of the Autism Consulting Service in Edmonton, Alberta, points out (in her book *Autism: A new understanding!*, 2000), an extension of our own world may be necessary before we can fully understand autism, a suspension of our own chatter and a willingness to listen:

> When we listen to those with autism, we discover a totally new picture of the condition. We find individuals who long for relationships with us, who have cognitive skills intact and are able to communicate with us in ways we never dreamed possible. It is definitely time for us to make the attempt to listen even more carefully in order to give up the hopelessness and despair that overwhelm so many of our parents and professionals. Hope for people with autism lies through acceptance and understanding.

Further reading

Attwood, Tony, *Asperger's Syndrome: A guide for parents and professionals*, Jessica Kingsley Publishers 1997.

Attwood, Tony, *Why Does Chris Do That?*, National Autistic Society 2002.

Baron-Cohen, Simon, and Bolton, Patrick, *Autism: The facts*, Oxford University Press 1998.

Carlson, Richard W., *My Brother Kevin Has Autism*, Writer's Club Press 2002.

Davis, Bill, *Breaking Autism's Barriers: A father's story*, Jessica Kingsley Publishers 2001.

Gillberg, Christopher, *A Guide to Asperger Syndrome*, Cambridge University Press 2002.

Gillingham, Gail, *Autism: Handle with care!*, Future Horizons 1995.

Gillingham, Gail, *Autism: A new understanding!*, Tacit Publishing 2000.

Grandin, Temple, *Thinking in Pictures: And other reports from my life with autism*, Bantam Books 1995.

Grandin, Temple, and Scariano, Margaret M., *Emergence: Labeled autistic*, Warner Books 1996.

Hamilton, Lynn R., and Rimland, Bernard, *Facing Autism: Giving parents reasons for hope and guidance for help*, Waterbrook Press 2000.

Jones, Vicky, et al., *New Horizons: A practical guide to organising family-based short breaks for people with autism*, Shared Care Network 1997 (see Useful addresses section for contact details).

Lawson, Wendy, *Understanding and Working with the Spectrum of Autism: An insider's view*, Jessica Kingsley Publishers 2001.

Lewis, Lisa, *Special Diets for Special Kids*, Future Horizons 1998.

Maurice, Catherine, *Let Me Hear Your Voice: A family's triumph over autism*, Fawcett Books 1994.

Romanowski Bashe, Patricia, and Kirby, Barbara L., *The OASIS Guide to Asperger Syndrome*, Crown Publishers 2001.

Sacks, Oliver, *The Man Who Mistook His Wife for a Hat*, Touchstone Books 1998.

Seroussi, Karyn, and Rimland, Bernard, *Unraveling the Mystery of*

Autism and Pervasive Developmental Disorder: A mother's story of research and recovery, Simon & Schuster 2000.

Shaw, William, *Biological Treatments for Autism and PDD*, Great Plains Laboratory Inc. 2001.

Wheeler, Maria, *Toilet Training for Individuals with Autism and Related Disorders*, Future Horizons 1998.

Willey, Liane Holliday, *Pretending to be Normal: Living with Asperger's Syndrome*, Jessica Kingsley Publishers 1999.

Wing, Lorna, et al., *The Autistic Spectrum: A parent's guide to understanding and helping your child*, Ulysses Press 2001.

Useful addresses

UK

National Autistic Society (NAS)
393 City Road
London EC1V 1NG
Tel: 020 7833 2299
Helpline: 0800 358 8667
Fax: 020 7833 9666
Website: <www.nas.org.uk>
E-mail: <nas@nas.org.uk> and <autismhelpline@nas.org.uk>
An excellent resource of exhaustive information and many links to
other websites.

Allergy Induced Autism
8 Hollie Lucas Road
King's Heath
Birmingham B13 0QL
Tel: 01733 331771 and 0121 444 6450
Website: <www.autismmedical.com>

AUTISM Independent UK
(Formerly SFTAH – Society For The Autistically Handicapped)
199–205 Blandford Avenue
Kettering
Northamptonshire NN16 9AT
Tel: 01536 523274
Fax: 01536 523274
Website: <www.autismuk.com>
E-mail: <autism@rmplc.co.uk>

Autism London
1 Floral Place
Northampton Grove
London N1 2FS
Tel: 020 7704 0501
Helpline: 020 7359 6070 (open Mon–Fri 2–5 p.m.)

Fax: 020 7704 2306
Website: <www.autismlondon.org.uk>
E-mail: <info@autismlondon.org.uk>

Autism Research Unit
School of Sciences (Health)
University of Sunderland
Sunderland SR2 7EE
Tel: 0191 510 8922
Fax: 0191 567 0429
Website: <http://osiris.sunderland.ac.uk/autism>
E-mail: <autism.unit@sunderland.ac.uk>
For information on the effects of vitamins and diet on autism.

Ainsworth's Homoeopathic Pharmacy
36 New Cavendish Street
London W1M 7LH
Tel: 020 7935 5330
Fax: 020 7486 4313
Website: <www.ainsworths.com>
E-mail: <mark.ainsworths@ukonline.co.uk>
For secretin therapy – pills or drops are available and cost from around £9.

British Association of Behavioural Optometrists
c/o Aquila Optometrists
72 High Street
Billericay
Essex CM12 9BS
Tel: 01277 624916
Fax: 01277 634150
Website: <www.babo.co.uk>
E-mail: <aquila72@aol.com>

British Society for Music Therapy
61 Church Hill Road
East Barnet
Hertfordshire EN4 8SY
Tel: 020 8441 6226
Fax: 020 8441 4118
Website: <www.bsmt.org>
E-mail: <info@bsmt.org>

Daily Life Therapy
Honormead Schools Limited
The Grange
Hospital Lane
Mickleover
Derby DE3 5DR
Tel: 01332 510951
Fax: 01332 512867
E-mail: <schooladmissions@honormead.btinternet.com>

Dog Aid (Assistance in Disability)
63 Parkville Highway
Whitmore Park
Coventry CV6 4HT
Tel: 024 7626 0584
Website: <www.dogaid.org.uk>
E-mail: <joy@dogaid.org.uk>
Helps people with disabilities to train their own dogs.

Dogs for the Disabled
The Frances Hay Centre
Blacklocks Hill
Banbury
Oxfordshire OX17 2BS
Tel: 01295 252600
Fax: 01295 252668
Website: <www.dogsforthedisabled.org>
E-mail: <info@dogsforthedisabled.org>

Hoffmann de Visme Foundation
Unit B
Lynton Road
London N8 8SL
Tel: 020 8342 7310
Fax: 020 8341 1235
Website: <www.hdvfoundation.org.uk>
E-mail: <mail@hdvfoundation.org.uk>

National Light and Sound Therapy Centre
80 Queen Elizabeth's Walk
London N16 5UQ
Tel: 020 8880 1269
Fax: 020 8809 5420
Website: <www.light-and-sound.co.uk>
E-mail: <zl@light-and-sound.co.uk>
For details of auditory integration therapy.

PEACH (Parents for the Early Intervention of Autism in Children)
The Brackens
London Road
Ascot
Berkshire SL5 8BE
Tel: 01344 882248
Fax: 01344 882391
Website: <www.peach.org.uk>
E-mail: <info@peach.org.uk>

PECS
Pyramid Educational Consultants UK Limited
Pavilion House
6 Old Steine
Brighton BN1 1EJ
Tel: 01273 609555
Fax: 01273 609556
Website: <www.pecs.org.uk>
E-mail: <pyramid@pecs.org.uk>

Shared Care Network
Units 63–66
Easton Business Centre
Felix Road
Bristol BS5 0HE
Tel: 0117 941 5361
Fax: 0117 941 5362
Website: <www.sharedcarenetwork.org.uk>
E-mail: <shared-care@bristol.ac.uk>
Can advise on short breaks.

USA

Asperger Syndrome Coalition of the US (ASC-U.S.)
PO Box 771
2020 Pennsylvania Avenue NW
Washington DC 20006
Tel: 866 427 7747
Website: <www.asperger.org>
E-mail: <info@asc-us.org>

Autism Network International (ANI)
PO Box 35448
Syracuse, NY 13235–5448
Website: <http://ani.autistics.org>
E-mail: <ani@autistics.org>
Autistic-run self-help organization.

Autism Research Institute
4182 Adams Avenue
San Diego
CA 92116
Tel/fax: 619 563 6840
Website: <www.autism.com/ari>

Autism Society of America (ASA)
7910 Woodmont Avenue
Suite 300
Bethesda
MD 20814 3067
Tel: 301 657 0881
Fax: 301 657 0869
Website: <www.autism-society.org>
E-mail: <info@autism-society.org>

Center for the Study of Autism
PO Box 4538
Salem
OR 97302
Website: <www.autism.org>
Also contact for the Society for Auditory Integration Training.

College of Optometrists in Vision Development
243 North Lindbergh Boulevard
Suite 310
St Louis
MO 63141
Tel: 314 991 4007 or 888 268 3770
Fax: 314 991 1167
Website: <www.covd.org/od/contact.html>
E-mail: <info@covd.org>

Daily Life Therapy
The Boston Higashi School
800 North Main Street
Randolph
MA 02368
Tel: 1781 961 0800
Fax: 1781 961 0888
Website: <www.bostonhigashi.org>
E-mail: <Wilkinson@bostonhigashi.org>

The Gray Center
2020 Raybrook SE
Suite 101
Grand Rapids, MI 49546
Tel: 616 954 9747
Fax: 616 954 9749
Website: <www.thegraycentcr.org>
E-mail: <info@thegraycenter.org>
For details of social stories.

Maap Services Inc. (More Able Autistic People)
PO Box 524
Crown Point
IN 46307
Tel: 219 662 1311
Fax: 219 662 0638
Website: <www.maapservices.org>
E-mail: <chart@netnitco.net>

Parents For Early Intervention (PFEI)
See Autism Society of America, above

Canada

Autism Society Canada
PO Box 65
Orangeville
Ontario L9W 2Z5
Tel: 519 942 8720
Fax: 519 942 3566
Website: <www.autismsocietycanada.ca>
E-mail: <info@autismsocietycanada.ca>

National Service Dogs (Canada)
PO Box 28009
Preston Postal Outlet
Cambridge
Ontario N3H 5N4
Tel: 519 662 4223
Fax: 519 662 4697
Website: <www.nsd.on.ca>
E-mail: <info@nsd.on.ca>

Websites

Autism Network for Dietary Intervention (ANDI)
Website: <www.AutismNDI.com>

Delacato International
Website: <www.delacato.net>

Division TEACCH
University of North Carolina
Website: <www.teacch.com/teacch.htm>
E-mail: <teacch@unc.edu>

Do2Learn
Website: <www.dotolearn.com>
E-mail: <contact@do2learn.com>
Website offering free picture cards to print out and use as communication tools for children with autism.

Dr Temple Grandin's work at Center for the Study of Autism
Website: <www.autism.org/contents.html#temple>

Facilitated Communication Institute
Syracuse University
Website: <http://soeweb.syr.edu/thefci>
E-mail: <fcstaff@sued.syr.edu>

INLV (independent living on the autistic spectrum)
Website: <www.inlv.demon.nl/internaut>
Online support for people with autism or Asperger syndrome.

Wendy Lawson's web page
Website: <www.mugsy.org/wendy/index2.htm>

Index